MARRIAGE VAMPIRE:
Living with a Narcissist

A Guide for Christian Women

MARRIAGE VAMPIRE:
Living with a Narcissist

A Guide for Christian Women

Clifton Fuller

Copyright

Disclaimer

Marriage Vampire:
Living with a Narcissist

This book's entire contents are based upon research conducted by the author unless otherwise noted. The publisher, authors, distributors, and bookstores only present this information for educational purposes.

This information is not intended to diagnose or prescribe medical or psychological conditions, nor does it claim to prevent, treat, mitigate, or cure such conditions; recommend specific information, products, or services as treatments of disease; provide diagnosis, care, treatment, or rehabilitation of individuals; or apply medical, mental health, or human development principles to provide diagnosing, treating, operating, or prescribing for any human disease, pain, injury, deformity or physical condition.

The information herein does not replace one-on-one relationships with a doctor, therapist, or qualified mental health professional. Therefore, the reader should be aware this information is not intended as medical advice but as a sharing of knowledge and information from the research and experience of the author.

Testimonials represent a cross-section of the range of results that appear to be typical with the information, products, or services. Results may vary depending upon use and commitment. This information is intended solely for expressive association purposes. The publisher/author encourages you to make your own medical and mental health decisions based on your research and partnership with a qualified mental health professional and physician. You alone are responsible if you choose to do anything based on what you read.

Scripture Quotations

Scripture quotations in *Marriage Vampire: Living with a Narcissist* are from the following Bible versions:

~ ~ ~

Note to Readers: If you are a teacher, English major, or editor, I'm not trying to taunt you with the punctuation you will find used in the various versions of the scriptures. Even though some punctuation may appear to be incorrect for today's standard punctuation rules, the punctuation utilized in this book is punctuation used in that specific version referenced (at least at the time that version was written). Try not to cringe. And if you find other errors my incredible editing team and I have missed, could you just pretend it's like scripture spellings and punctuations of the time...and let me get away with it? I'd greatly appreciate that.:) Clifton Fuller

Dedication

I dedicate this book to clients who taught me so much about things I was supposed to know already. Your strength, search for answers, and determination have been an inspiration. I saw firsthand the changes you made to improve your lives and your family's lives.

I dedicate this book to all the courageous women who learned to stand up for themselves and hold on fiercely to their inner strength. This includes my precious mother, Mary Fuller, who refused to admit defeat. Instead, she walked a difficult path, with little more than determination, to both live a better life and provide a better life for her children. Her struggles taught her seven children that we could be strong, no matter what the world might dish out or the complex challenges we would meet. Her inner strength became ours.

And to those women who are still fighting to do what is right and trying to listen to the voice inside them that persistently keeps telling them they are "holy and loved"—you are the true champions of the world!

Epigraph

*"but those who hope in the LORD
will renew their strength.
They will soar on wings like eagles;
they will run and not grow weary,
they will walk and not be faint."*
(Isiah 40:31, NIV)

Table of Contents

Foreword

Out of the thousands of books that come our way every year on marriage and the family, typically only a few grab our attention and instantly stand out from the crowd. I predict Clifton Fuller's *Marriage Vampire* will be one of those writings. To begin with, Fuller addresses a topic that few have treated but that all of us know exists. We may not know the people by their clinical name—Narcissistic Personal Disorder (also known as "NPD")—but we all know someone who fits this diagnosis. Some may know them all too well, as a fiancé, spouse, parent, or friend.

Another reason this book will quickly gain acceptance and popularity is the direct and down-to-earth way Clifton writes. I have known Clifton for more than 40 years. He is an extraordinarily skilled therapist who has a talent for telling it like it is, with an often folksy and humorous style that nevertheless leaves no doubt about the message. Clifton has personal experience within his own family of the abusive nature of a marriage vampire. I will let him tell you about it in his own words. As you will quickly see, the man knows what he is talking about from a personal and professional perspective.

Finally, and most importantly, Clifton approaches this complex issue from a biblical perspective, bringing to bear Scriptures that heal and give direction to our lives, even in the most challenging circumstances. Clifton's Christian walk adds even more to the authenticity of his message.

Once you start this book, you will not put it down. Let the adventure begin!

Royce Money, Ph.D.
Chancellor and former President, Abilene Christian University

Preface

Narcissistic Personality Disorder is a serious disorder, and not every egotistical, selfish, or arrogant person is a narcissist.

Narcissist Personality Disorders are challenging to diagnose, even for mental health professionals. It requires a knowledge of their actual behaviors and patterns, not what a narcissist may know about themselves (as they are often unaware, or even dishonest, about their behaviors or habits).

It has become common for people to use the label "narcissist" as a weapon.

As a therapist, clients may ask me to diagnose their partner if they believe they are a narcissist. I cannot do so without seeing the partner. Once I have seen their partner, a diagnosis might be appropriate but is not based upon a partner's conclusion as to the diagnosis. I can confirm the traits described, but this is not diagnosing a person based on firsthand knowledge of their partner's behavior.

My goal for those in a possible narcissistic relationship is to focus on the behaviors they must deal with to succeed in a complicated relationship, no matter what the diagnosis may be for any person involved.

I may tell an actual client if their partner may show narcissistic traits, but the book intends to help the clients (or readers) heal themselves, not their partners. You cannot control another person, but you can control yourself, your reactions, and your beliefs. This book is for you, not them.

Acknowledgments

"and let us consider how to stir up
one another to love and good works..."
(Hebrews 10:24, RSV)

I first want to thank the love of my life, my wife, Jeanne. She has always believed in me, thought I could and should write a book, and has supported me continuously in this and every other endeavor we approached along our journey in life together. She is my joy, my inspiration, and the one who brought happiness to a Houston boy who had never experienced good things in life before meeting her.

Special thanks to our college friends, Don and Chris Wise, who were such an encouragement, allowed us to rely on their knowledge and skills, and were invaluable help; and to Anne Severance, who brought more insight to this venture than anyone could imagine.

Special thanks and "Wow!" to Sarah Carlson, Grace Michael, and Jonathan Fuller, editors extraordinaire, whose wisdom and skills increased clarity and understanding from the original manuscript's revision to the final product. You were such a blessing to us in this endeavor, not only as skilled wordsmiths and knowledgeable writers but also as delightful people with whom we have had the honor to work.

Thanks to the many frustrated teachers who attempted to educate me and who are surely now scratching their heads or rolling in their graves at the thought that this dyslexic class clown would be able to quit eating paste long enough to write a book.

Special thanks to my fifth-grade teacher, Mrs. Floyd Burkett, from Houston, TX, who put a cart filled with encyclopedias next to my desk, knowing I struggled to read but hoping the pictures in those books would encourage me to try. Even though I had difficulty reading, she recognized my unusual ability to memorize. I went from being the class clown to a teacher's pet (which I'd never been before to any teacher or in any class). She cast me as the main character in her yearly theatre performance, and it was in her class, as I recited all four verses of the Star-Spangled Banner and performed, that I received the first intoxicating gift of public applause from peers and adults.

Special thanks to Dr. Chris Willerton (my college professor who taught freshman English and read so fast with his speed-reading skills that I passed his course with flying colors).

Special thanks to Royce Money, who became my role model of what a Christian marriage therapist should be, who believed in me and my therapeutic skills, who encouraged me as a graduate student, and continues to inspire me to this day.

These educators and mentors were among those who became life-changers for me. Educators and people who care can change lives and inspire people they may never even realize they have helped. I am indebted to all of you.

Last but not least, thanks to the creators of spell-checking software programs. You make life so much easier.

~ ~ ~

Special Thanks to the following photographers and design programs (in order of appearance in the book)

- Book Front Cover (Sarah Douglas, Full of Grace Marketing). Book Back Cover (Design: Sarah Douglas, Full of Grace Marketing; Kat Carey, DarkRoomFoto, Clifton Fuller photograph)

- Victoria Labadie, (Fotonomada, Pexels, Getty Images, Canva Design, Introduction, Woman at Door)

- Laura Meinhardt (Pexels, Canva Design, Castle in Fog, Chapter 1)

- Monstera, (Pexels, Children, Devil, Angel, Chapter 1)

- Pedro Figueras, (Pexels, Person in Fog, Chapter 2)

- Zimmytws (Getty Images, Canva Design, Chapter 3, Lies)

- Kieferpix (Getty Images, Canva Design, Book-Heart, Chapter 4)

- Levranii (Canva Design, Target and Arrows, Chapter 4)

- Valentyn Volkov (Getty Images, Canva Design, Oyster, Chapter 5)

- Canva Design (Three Levels of Communication, Chapter 5)

- Teiro and Nikitabuida (Canva Design, Woman with Raised Arms, Shield, Chapter 6)

- Nejron (Canva Design, Warrior Woman, Chapter 6)

- Svitlana Barsukova (Getty Images, Canva Design, Woman-No, Chapter 7)

- Bowie15 (Getty Images, Canva Design, Woman-Fist, Chapter 8)

- Brett Jordon (Pexels, Canva Design, Let It Go, Chapter 9)

- Tutye (Getty Images, Canva Design, Woman Breaking Free of Chains, Chapter 9)

- Monkey Business (Canva Designs, Thoughtful Woman, Chapter 10)

- Kali9 (Getty Images, Canva Design, Women Exercising, Chapter 10)

- Makidotyn (Getty Images, Canva Design, Woman With Salad, Chapter 10)

- Kali9 (Getty Images, Canva Design, Two Women Laughing, Chapter 10)

- Banana Stock (Photo Images, Canva Design, Woman with Medication, Chapter 10)

- Wavebreakmedia (Getty Images, Canva Design, Woman Reading, Chapter 10)

- Nicexray (Getty Images, Canva Design, Woman and Music, Chapter 10)

- Pixland (Photo Images, Canva Design, Group of Women, Chapter 11)

- Kat Carey (DarkRoomFoto, Clifton Fuller photograph, About the Author)

Introduction

"For people will be lovers of self, lovers of money, proud, arrogant, abusive, disobedient to their parents, ungrateful, unholy, heartless, unappeasable, slanderous, without self-control, brutal, not loving good, treacherous, reckless, swollen with conceit, lovers of pleasure rather than lovers of God, having the appearance of godliness, but denying its power.
Avoid such people."
(II Timothy 3:1-5, ESV)

Marriage Vampire is a book about Narcissistic Personality Disorder and its effect on intimate relationships.

Even though I will refer to individuals with this disorder as "marriage vampires," as it—and they—certainly affect marriages, narcissists also affect the lives of those around them, from business to church, to extended families, to friends, to government. I have worked with this type of disorder for many decades in my counseling practice and have seen the heartbreak and confusion the narcissistic personality has on others.

Why do I refer to narcissists as "marriage vampires?"

Like the mythical creatures known as vampires, Narcissists drain another person's life energy. You may not even realize this personality type exists until you have been bitten, impacted, or seriously damaged by a marriage vampire. Narcissists can severely hurt or even destroy their marriages and relationships with their children, friends, family, and all with whom they come in contact.

Why do I refer to narcissists using the pronoun "he" rather than "she?"

Even though narcissists are occasionally women, the most significant number of narcissists are men. That is reflected in research data and my personal experience in my counseling practice.

I have witnessed self-confident, exuberant, and happy women become shells of their former selves because of the abusive behavior of a marriage vampire. I know the extensive amount of therapy it takes to gently help these women move out of their prison-like state and back into the whole and happy life they deserve.

I do not want any unsuspecting person to suffer the pain a marriage vampire will inflict. That is why it is crucial to identify a marriage vampire and understand how they operate!

The mental health field knows all about them, as narcissists characteristics were outlined in the *Diagnostic and Statistical Manual of Mental Disorders (DSM 5)* for years.

God explicitly warns us about this type of personality in the Bible, which extensively details these destructive personalities. It also teaches us how to combat their dangerous lies, mind-games, and twisted reality.

I will share practical steps to take if you are already in a relationship with, or are married to, a marriage vampire or if you are attempting to counsel or help someone in such a relationship.

God has a loving view of each of his children, which is quite different from the negative perception you will hear from the mouth of a marriage vampire. You must understand that God provides the ability for you to survive the marriage vampire's oppressive and fiery darts, purposely designed to imprison you in ungodly subjection. However, the most important thing that I want you to know is that God loves you beyond anything you could ever imagine.

This is not a book about helping the marriage vampire as much as it is about helping *you*. It's essential to understand the characteristics of a marriage vampire and how to deal with them as effectively as possible.

The Beginning of the Journey

Two parents once came to my office, tearfully asking for help for their daughter, Linda, whom they had brought to the session. After a lengthy discussion with the parents about Linda and Linda's husband, as Linda sat there silently, I began listing characteristics of narcissists. I asked if they had seen any of those patterns with him.

The parents hadn't. But when I specifically asked their depressed Linda, she began to share details of her life and marriage, of which her parents did not know. They were heartbroken to hear what had been happening, as well as by the fact their daughter had not felt she could share these things with them, even though they had always held a remarkably close relationship. Because the truth was, Linda was married to a marriage vampire, and he was sucking the life out of her.

"Why didn't someone tell us these people existed?" the parents asked me. "If we had only known, we could have helped our daughter avoid making the worst mistake of her life. You've got to warn others about these people!"

I am dyslexic, so writing a book is certainly not something that comes easily for me. Yet, as I have had many similar requests, this book became my attempt to reach out beyond the walls of my office and warn the unsuspecting.

If you can spot the early warning signals of Narcissistic Personality Disorder (NPD), you will know not to say "Yes" to a narcissist's charming yet deceptive advances. Instead, you will be empowered to recognize a marriage vampire, say "No," and prevent a lifelong recipe for disaster.

I have included stories of shell-shocked victims to help you realize other intelligent women have also walked through this fog and survived.

I also want to emphasize this point: Not every troubled marriage is because a vampire hides in it! I do not want people to see a marriage vampire hiding behind every tree. But marriage vampires exist, and if you or a loved one runs into one, you need to know if they are wolves in sheep's clothing from the beginning of a relationship. It might help protect your future, and it may even save your life or the life of a child, friend, or family member!

If you see yourself or a person you care about on the cover of this book, do not put it down. A door is opening for you.

I will attempt to help you walk through the door as you find the way out of the marriage vampire's world of smoke and mirrors. I hope that this book, put into action, will become not only a healing balm for the wounded but a foundation to help you stand, to be a catalyst for action, and a doorway into a fruitful and happy future.

Clifton Fuller, LCSW, LPC, LMFT
Marriage & Family Therapist
San Antonio, Texas
CliftonFullerCounseling.com

1

Prince Charming or Count Dracula?

"Beware of those who come to you in sheep's clothing but inwardly are ravenous wolves."
(Matthew 7:15, NKJV)

Prince Charming or Count Dracula?

You may have read books or watched movies such as *Cinderella, Sleeping Beauty,* and *The Little Mermaid* as a little girl. These fairy tales all end the same way: a couple falls in love, overcomes a crisis, gets married, and lives happily ever after. She becomes a princess; he is the handsome prince. We last see them at the altar; the ending credits only show their happiness and the assumption that

they will always be together. We conclude they will never face another crisis and will go through life with joy, as the ending crescendos into cheerful music with birds happily singing in the background.

Those make-believe stories somehow creep into our sub-conscious, and we begin to look for that "special person" with whom we believe we can live happily ever after. This may have been your dream. You were selective; you were cautious; you prepared yourself all your life to be that perfect princess with whom your handsome prince would fall madly in love, treasure, and value.

You thought you found the perfect partner; the marriage took place.

You may have had niggling warnings or questioned unresolved issues but attributed those to wedding jitters or miscommunication. Yet you had confidence any difficulties would work out on their own as you began the journey of life together.

Every marriage has difficulties that can make it stronger and thrive if partners work together to address them while valuing the other during the process. But you began to realize this is not the case in your marriage. You are not working on issues together.

One day, you wake up and look with longing at the wedding picture hidden in the back of the drawer, vaguely remembering that happy bride, full of life, vitality, and dreams, thrilled to be marrying her Prince Charming.

You realize this is not your reality. Rather than being married to that once wonderful man, you find yourself trapped in a relationship that is no longer loving and caring. For Christian women who believe that marriage is forever, feelings of hopelessness and despair may be present to an even greater degree.

It seems that no matter what you do, it's never right. You may be ashamed that everything you thought you knew about marriage and being a good wife is not working. You feel like a failure. All your energy, confidence, and even personality are gone.

What happened to that girl so full of hope and dreams? Where did you go wrong? Why are you ashamed and un-willing to tell anyone about your real life, especially those you love the most? You know there is no way your friends, associates, or even family members would ever believe your Camelot marriage is a facade or that your perfect catch of a husband would ever treat you the way he does.

You may not yet realize it, but you may be married to a marriage vampire. You are a slave to him, and he is slowly draining all your self-esteem and worth to feed his un-quenchable need to sustain his ego.

The attacks on you are never-ending. Each day your hap-piness, fulfillment, and joy drain because a husband dom-inates and controls your life—even what you think and how you feel about yourself.

He is bigger, stronger, and louder. He will become enraged if you dare suggest he is wrong about anything he says or does. You are just too weary, too weak to resist or even to fight back. What happened?

~ ~ ~

When Linda's parents called me, they were frantic. They were so worried about their daughter they were willing to do whatever it took to get help for her immediately.

Married a little more than two years, Linda had changed from a happy, confident, outgoing young woman to a with-drawn, insecure shell of her former self. She had lost a great deal of weight, was tired all the time, and couldn't give a straight answer to any question her parents asked. She spoke to them less and less and hadn't visited in a year—there was never a convenient time, and she always had to "get back" with them when offered an invitation to meet. When they asked what was wrong, she always replied, "Nothing." Everything was "just fine."

Linda's parents knew that things were not "fine." After one alarming phone call, they decided to surprise Linda with a visit, thinking to cheer her up and discover what was happening in her life.

When they saw her, they were stunned. She looked like a shell-shocked refugee with desperation on her face. She was afraid to go anywhere.

They insisted. "C'mon honey; we're taking you to get something to eat." Linda reluctantly went, but she was tense.

They wondered what had happened to her. How had she changed so fast? Why hadn't she asked for help? Gradually, the story unfolded.

Before marriage, her husband had been so charming and caring, devoted and debonair. Yet after they'd married, he had begun to reject and push Linda away. He had quickly destroyed her confidence, her self-image, and even her identity, to the point that she saw herself as a "nobody." This young woman, once so popular and outgoing in college and graduating at the top of her class, seeming to have the world by the tail, had been swept off her feet by a classmate. It was all too good to be true. They married quickly, and he whisked her off to a big city to live happily ever after.

Bit by bit, day by day, this man had increasingly sucked out more of this woman's lifeblood through his demeaning behavior and control. The friends they used to hang out with became forbidden and were no longer good enough to spend time with. He threw away all of Linda's clothing, demanding she wear only the clothes he selected. She was no longer allowed to attend the church where they had been married unless he was with her, eventually attending so infrequently they rarely attended at all. He demanded a detailed accounting of how she spent her time when they were not together. He had become so critical of her actions—nothing she did was right—and she could never do enough to please him.

Linda wondered what had happened to bring about this drastic change. Was it something she did? Was it something she said? Was she losing her mind? The pendulum had swung so dramatically that she felt dizzy—disoriented—as if she were in a fog. Her husband's response? He was pointing out that she was dumb! She brought out her old annuals, and report cards to prove to him—and herself—that she was intelligent and attractive...or at least had been at one time.

When she tried to reason with him, he would throw a temper tantrum, yell, or break things within his reach, even about the smallest of matters. If they went anywhere, he openly flirted with other women in front of Linda and would tell her how unattractive she'd let herself become. He brought pornography home and watched it in front of her. He said, "You need to do this to take care of my needs." He justified his behavior by saying, "Your goody-goody ways don't satisfy me anymore."

She felt violated and ashamed of what she had become, yet she felt hopeless and trapped. Her husband had warned her that if she told anyone about their marriage, he would make her regret it.

She felt defeated. She wished she could "go to sleep and never wake up." Feeling this way is common ideation for suicidal Christian women. Only dead people go to sleep and never wake up.

Linda began to tell her parents what her life had become. They were alarmed and immediately made an appointment for the three of them to meet in a counseling session.

Once I learned of Linda's situation, I knew she would have to brace herself for what was coming next. As soon as her husband discovered she had confided in her parents, it would be World War III. If she had given in and had gone back to him at this point, her parents might never have had an opportunity to intervene again. It was easy to see these parents had saved their daughter's life.

I told them the first step was immediately scheduling an appointment with a physician to treat Linda for depression. She was sleep-deprived and had been without any peace for so long that she was incapable of logical thought. She did not have the mental ability or physical stamina to fully comprehend or confront what had happened and what would continue to happen to her.

Linda's parents knew time was of the essence. They made an appointment with a physician for Linda. She began to receive the rest she so desperately needed. They also made immediate appointments so all three could obtain intensive counseling, both individually and in family therapy.

Do Marriage Vampires Exist?

As Linda and her parents gathered in my office, I began to share information about NPD and revealed the truth of Linda's situation. I shared with them that marriage vampires do not prey on weak people; they prey on people with weaknesses.

We all have weaknesses and shortcomings. A marriage vampire believes he has no flaws, but he will listen as you confess yours. You don't realize that he never shares his weaknesses but instead is quietly collecting the information you share about yourself. He builds a portfolio against you from your honest and intimate conversations about your family, feelings, weaknesses, inabilities, and past regrets, which you shared with him in confidence. Instead of safeguarding your heart, as a caring husband promises to and should do, he will threaten to reveal your weaknesses, using them as weapons against you whenever he likes, such as when you have an opinion that differs from his. He uses any means, including your confessions, to justify his conclusions and actions.

He may say, "You told me you failed and labeled yourself a failure. I agree with you. Why should I listen to someone who is an admitted failure? I cannot believe I married you! I must be a saint! Look at you. You're despicable!"

Linda's parents were genuinely shocked.

"This is the first time anyone has ever suggested there are people like this," they said.

Linda cried and said, "I thought I was going crazy."

"These guys are like vampires in the movies," I told her, as I have told clients for years. "No one seems to know they exist until they've been bitten by one."

Linda experienced the effects of what it feels like when a marriage vampire sinks his fangs into his victim.

Where do these disorders come from? We don't know how these personalities form, but mental health and medical professionals believe people with these personalities are born as "normal" as the rest of us. Then, somewhere along the way, something happens that leads NPDs to develop distinctive traits so different from ours that it is hard for us to believe they come from the same planet.

How Vampires Form

Personality disorders are the medical and mental health profession's attempts to describe groups of "symptoms or traits." Unlike schizophrenia or bipolar disorder, which are biological illnesses, the NPD's traits are powerful defensive structures used to protect oneself from hurt, pain, or judgment.

Theoretically, mental health professionals believe narcissistic personality disorders form through a child's early experiences, theoretically during the terrible twos. People with NPD cannot tell you what caused the changes in their behavior because they have always "been this way." No one remembers what happens that early in one's life, and we cannot ask a two-year-old to describe emotional responses. If a personality disorder forms, we only know that in hindsight.

I tell my clients that if you have a personality disorder at thirty, you had it at three.

For those of us who have children, we knew that we'd be judged by our children's appropriate or inappropriate behaviors when we were new parents.

If a child was ill-mannered or ill-behaved, others suggested we were "bad" parents. If a child failed or had too many difficulties in school, others considered us a family with problems because we had a defective child.

If a child was well-behaved, performed well, or even excelled, then we were considered "good" parents. We were a model family with a model child. What we weren't told is the truth. There are no perfect parents, no perfect children, no perfect families, and no perfect people.

Counselors believe vampires form when a mother attempts to create a perfect child. To have this perfect child, a mother may feel pressured to give the child whatever he wants, whenever he wants it. It is one thing to want your child to do well. It is quite another issue when you think you can create a perfect child without flaws.

Not only do we put pressure on ourselves as parents, but society, family, church, friends, peers, and schools also add pressure to conform, behave or act in what they perceive to be appropriate or acceptable ways.

My Child Is Perfect

So, what happens during the terrible twos when a child begins to say "No" and attempts to individuate from the mother (or another primary caregiver) who believes a child can be perfect.

Mom (or the caregiver) will not let the child be independent. Otherwise, he will do things that embarrass her or show others she is not in control—and she feels she must control every aspect of the child's behavior.

She will constantly tell the child, "You're great, you're smart, you're wonderful, and you do everything right." She will be sickeningly sweet. "Oh, honey, you can't climb the tree! You might be injured. No, you cannot do what the other boys are doing. I'm afraid you'll get lost or be injured." The mother is overwhelmingly positive with the child; however, when he attempts to individuate from her, she punishes him by saying, "Now see, everyone will know how stupid you are," or "They will know you are a failure. If you are a failure, then I am a failure, and I will never let that happen."

The child now only has two frames of reference: he is either perfect or worthless. The child thinks he is either the prince who does everything right or the village idiot who does everything wrong. The child learns psychological tricks to cover inadequacies because he finds it too painful to be without value.

This is the first step in forming the survival instincts of a narcissistic personality. In other words, the first steps to creating a vampire.

A Black-and-White World

Those with NPD live in a black-and-white world. As adults, they assume the role of the positive voice of their mother. "I'm so great; I'm so pretty; I'm so perfect!" They are unable to acknowledge any error or a simple mistake. If you say, "You bought the wrong book," they will say, "No, I didn't!" They believe they cannot and do not do anything wrong. A marriage vampire genuinely believes he is always right, and if you say he isn't, you are attacking him for no reason.

These egotistical charmers, who abuse others, have been this way all their lives and do not see anyone else's needs. They never grew up; they just got older. The marriage vampire's mother would say to his wife, "He's just himself. He throws those temper tantrums all the time. Just do what he says, give in, and tell him you were wrong." In the abuser's mind, he does not do the things he does to hurt us; the things he does happen to cause real pain and drive us nuts! He does not even know he has these traits. He will deny them, but the characteristics will show up in his behavior.

When people describe the NPD's behaviors to me, I try to help them see the pattern. For example, if you have a shell, four legs, and you can quickly pull your body into that shell, you are a turtle. If you are a turtle with specific markings, such as a pointy nose and mean disposition, you are a snapping turtle.

Narcissistic DSM IV Criteria [*]

The *Diagnostic and Statistical Manual of Mental Disorders-IV*, the manual used to diagnose mental health disorders, lists nine traits for the NPD.

---

[*] DSM V Criteria diagnosing personality disorders were listed in the 2012 edition.

The disorder has a pervasive pattern of grandiosity (in fantasy or behavior), a need for admiration, and a lack of empathy, beginning by early adulthood and present in a variety of contexts, as indicated by five (or more) of the following:

1) Has a grandiose sense of self-importance (e.g., exaggerates achievements and talents, expects recognition as superior without commensurate achievements).

2) Preoccupied with fantasies of unlimited success, power, brilliance, beauty, or ideal love.

3) Believes that they are special and unique and can only be understood by, or associate with, other special or high-status people (or institutions).

4) Requires excessive admiration.

5) Has a sense of entitlement (i.e., unreasonable expectations of especially favorable treatment or automatic compliance with their expectations).

6) Is interpersonally exploitative (i.e., takes advantage of others to achieve their own ends).

7) Lacks empathy and is unwilling to recognize or identify with the feelings and needs of others.

8) Is often envious of others or believes that others are envious of them.

9) Shows arrogant, haughty behaviors or attitudes.

If a person has five of these nine traits, the DSM manual indicates it may reflect a narcissistic personality disorder. Which five, you ask? It doesn't matter—any five of the nine. What if the person has only four? Well, that person is not technically classified as NPD, but they would have enough of the characteristics to make someone's life miserable.

Both men and women have this disorder. However, the most significant percentage of people with NPDs are male. These traits and the following stories apply to both male and female vampires.

But first—back up! Take another look at the seventh bullet point in the list above. It revolves around *empathy.*

Empathy is the Key!

Empathy is an essential trait that vampires lack. Empathy is the ability to understand how others feel, how others respond to what is happening to them, and what others need. *Empathy is the opposite of selfishness.*

A marriage vampire's behavior becomes highly manipulative. He will do anything and everything to obtain what he wants, what he needs, and whatever makes him look good. A vampire's mantra is "Me! Me! Me!"

The basis of our faith is to "...Love the Lord your God with all your heart, and with all your soul, and with all your strength, and with all your mind; and your neighbor as yourself." (Luke 10:27, RSV)

Without empathy, you cannot love your neighbor, enemy, or wife. The vampire does not understand these concepts, no matter how charming he may be. Charm is not the same as love—charm is public relations. It is presentation and spin. Vampires are charming but are not loving. Anyone who falls for their facade will eventually realize the vastness of that difference. You can go to charm school, but there is no empathy school.

In the Bible, Peter tells us that we should have the following traits:

"Finally, all of you, have unity of spirit, sympathy, love for one another, a tender heart, and a humble mind. Do not repay evil for evil or abuse for abuse." (1 Peter 3:8-9, NRSV)

Vampires cannot pull this off without the ability to understand and respond to others. They must be able to get outside themselves and care about someone else. Vampires only care about their own needs. They lack the milk of human kindness. They have no empathy, no compassion, no tender heart, and no love for others. They have no love for you. But they can fake it.

All con men know that sincerity is the key. If you can fake that, you have it made. Vampires can fake empathy, compassion, and any other positive trait. Unlike ordinary people, they can do it well enough and long enough to hook almost anyone. It is the key to their success, and they do it without effort. It is just the way they are made. *That is why we call it a disorder.*

2

Horror Stories

*"...the hatred he hated her with was greater
than the love with which he loved her..."*
(II Samuel 13:15, RSV)

He drives up in his status car, flashes his Rolex, and steps into the spotlight, drawing attention to himself. The trouble is, he may be so charming and likable that you cannot help being intrigued. You may find yourself joining the crowd that forms around him.

Some marriage vampires are willing to work tirelessly to achieve whatever it takes to become world-famous, whether in fantasy or reality. He will also most likely have succumbed to the God complex. If he is a lawyer, he will have the most sensational cases. If he is a dentist, his clientele includes TV and movie stars. If he is a politician, he will know all the right people and schmooze his way to the top. If the medical profession is his field, he will have saved more lives, been on the trail of the cure for a dreaded disease, and otherwise have distinguished himself in the medical profession. At least, that is what he will tell himself and others.

There is no end to his magnetism because he appears intelligent, attractive, and charismatic. He attracts people mystically. He will say the right words, make the right moves, and create an aura that magically mesmerizes all those in his path if he turns that powerful personality on others.

This is especially true if he's interested in more than a platonic relationship with you. You may be a goner before you can do anything to protect yourself. You may think, I am so lucky. Why has he chosen me?

When the marriage vampire is on a roll, you will hear him tell fascinating stories, liberally laced with the names of famous and desirable people. He can be so convincing that you will be positive he is the most amazing and influential person you have ever met. Where has this guy been all your life?

What you may miss is that he demands all the attention, all the time. It may feel as if you cannot catch your breath—that somehow, he has sucked the very air from the room. The spell he is spinning around his audience may make you oblivious to the fact that a lethal weapon has been unleashed—and that you are the target.

Because the marriage vampire considers himself so special, he feels he deserves the company of other prestigious people. When he finally notices other individuals, he wants to make sure they are good enough to hang out with him. He will scope out the most popular, beautiful, talented, and independent woman in the immediate vicinity. After he has captured such a woman, he seeks to dominate her, making him feel like he is dominating his mother.

I'll share horror stories that illustrate the marriage vampire's wiles.

Ken and Barbie

One of the clients who sought my counsel before marriage was a young woman who excelled in her professional studies, only to fall for a marriage vampire in her personal life. Here is her story:

They met in dental school. He was the "Ken" of their class, and she was the "Barbie." Their friends insisted they would be "perfect" together. He was, as advertised—handsome, bright, charming, articulate, and confident. She was beautiful, intelligent, confident, and well-liked. They both had high expectations for themselves. They set out to graduate at the top of their class to obtain the pick of the job placements. Of course, they also anticipated the financial security and prestige their profession offered along with their aspirations.

He was so romantic, but he did not tell her anything she had not heard before. "You're so beautiful ... so smart ... so funny." Same old lines she'd heard many times before. Though, he did better than the others to appeal to her pride. She believed she deserved a man like him—a winner who would have it all. He talked about how right they were for each other, how he wanted her, and that they should not wait any longer to hook up for keeps. To her, it was apparent they were meant to be together.

More than one man had fallen in love with her. It is just that she had never been willing to let herself fall for anyone. But this guy? He seemed special. This must be the real thing. They did have similar goals and values—their classes, their peers, and their future. They worked hard, and they were committed.

They spent time together at her house, studying and communicating late into the evening. He began sleeping at her place instead of going back to his apartment. He convinced her that they might be the perfect couple and hinted at a future together. He then moved in with her, and they began planning for a life of shared dreams that had a strong potential of coming true.

One day, Ken and Barbie were working out together at a gym. She noticed that he was moving from one apparatus to another, flexing his muscles, and showing off for a group of first-year college girls standing nearby. "Hey, you ladies come here often?" he asked.

They began a light conversation with him. Later, Barbie made an off-handed remark that let him know she didn't appreciate his behavior, flirting with other women and flaunting it in her face. He was shocked and could not believe she would think such a thing, much less say it!

Seeing his response, Barbie quickly apologized. They returned to her apartment, and things appeared to continue as before.

Weeks later, Ken said, "Let's have dinner at a fancy restaurant tonight. I have something to tell you." Barbie was thrilled because she thought he would ask her to marry him. They went to dinner. It was wonderful. At the end of the meal, she reminded Ken that he had said he wanted to tell her something important.

"You're not the one," he remarked casually.

Barbie was shocked. "Why? What had happened? What had she done?" she asked.

"We have too much conflict," he said.

Barbie thought to herself: This is not my first rodeo, and if this is too much conflict, I will not be riding in his parade anymore! Barbie had been in other relationships, and if one critical comment was too much, she knew this relationship would never work. Ken was just too fragile. She quickly gathered her thoughts and asked him, "So when are you moving out?"

Ken was surprised. "Who said anything about moving out?" he asked. Ken had laid down his rules, and Barbie did not go for it. In his mind, it was time for her to become his subject, and she should respond to his authority. He expected her to say, "Oh, please, Ken, don't go! I will do anything you want. I understand now that you will always expect me to apologize and ask for forgiveness if I don't do exactly what you want. I will do my best to meet your expectations. I promise never to disagree with you again!"

Fortunately, Barbie's self-esteem was still in good enough shape that she was able to end this relationship before walking down the aisle or going into business with him. Barbie had just escaped the clutches of a potential marriage vampire who expected complete authority over her and wanted no conflict or confrontation—ever. If she had given in, begged him to stay, and married this knucklehead, she would have set herself up for a lifetime of groveling.

Jack and Janice

A furious woman stormed into my office one day. Janice had been married for only a few months, but boy was she mad! After she calmed down, her story began to unfold. As this was a second marriage for both, she wanted to get it right this time.

Janice owned an extraordinarily successful small business selling high-end clothing. Jack was a tall, dark, handsome, retired stockbroker. He had wined and dined her during their courtship, taking her to expensive romantic getaways. During their dating, he explained to Janice that he had received a severance agreement retirement and was independently wealthy. In Janice's mind, this translated into lifelong security.

Following a short engagement, they were married.

Immediately Jack began "helping" Janice with her business. Because of his credentials, she handed over the financial decision-making to him.

One day, her outside auditing firm called to inform her that her company was losing money. Janice went to Jack. "What's going on?" she asked him.

"Nothing ... and I'm surprised you'd ask," he said. "And a little hurt, too. If you call off your money guy and let me manage things, I can fix it. Don't you trust me?"

Janice shook her head and walked away. She was too sharp to buy into his spiel. This situation drove her crazy, so she started looking more deeply into the books, even questioning her husband's motives. There could only be two conclusions in her mind: Jack either had little business ability and was naive to the damage he was doing, or he was stealing from her.

Where was the money going? Jack was independently wealthy, wasn't he? She soon found out that his "independent wealth" was gone, spent trying to impress her on their dates. She did something everyday folks should do when they want answers.

She consulted his past employer, a well-respected Fortune 500 company, to find out about their golden boy. They were hesitant to talk about his employment and said they would speak to her only if she signed a non-disclosure agreement. To her horror, the golden parachute retirement was, in fact, a way for them to get rid of Jack discreetly after learning he had been embezzling funds. The board felt it was best not to admit they had hired a thief to protect their money. They did not report it because this crime would have brought negative attention to their company, lowered their stock value, and revealed their lack of ability to recognize fraud. But that's not the entire story.

Unfortunately for this marriage vampire, his true colors surfaced a little too early for him to bleed Janice dry financially completely. But unfortunately, when Janice took her discoveries to the police, she soon learned that "Jack" wasn't even her husband's real name. He was merely a shadow with more than a dozen aliases. His rap sheet included fraud warrants in two states.

The officers she met with paused, looked at each other, then back at Janice. "Sorry, ma'am," one of them said. "Your husband probably forgot to mention that he is currently married to several other women."

Janice was shocked. She could not believe what he had done to her. But it could have been even worse. When asked, she had no problem giving the police his exact location. By the way, "Jack" now has a new permanent residence.

Back in my office, I could see her sadness and despair. This woman was smart, savvy, and no novice to the wiles of the world. But this guy had caught her off guard and almost destroyed her life's work, along with her confidence in herself and her ability to trust others.

Thank goodness she found out quickly and exposed this vampire to the light. If she had not, he would have finished her off, hopped in his car, and driven into the sunset on his way to his next innocent victim.

If you are fascinated by someone who might turn out to be your future mate, you will want to know everything about him. A marriage vampire will be elusive, giving you only partial answers. He will usually paint himself in glowing colors while downplaying the roles of others in his life. If you question him or attempt to draw him out further, he will either clam up or change the subject, and this moment of truth will skid to an abrupt halt. That should be your cue to get off the ride.

The marriage vampire is a smooth talker. You will come away from an encounter with him believing he's a saint. If he does share any defeats that may have previously occurred—a business failure, a broken relationship, a bankruptcy—he will frame it in such terms that you'll believe it could not have been his fault. He will have you convinced you are the favored one with whom he has chosen to share these tidbits.

It is also true that marriage vampires successfully siphon off the successes of others. NPDs perceive they are deserving of everything *you* have—and that you should willingly give everything to them on a silver platter.

Lance and Faith

After immigrating to the United States following World War II, Faith was the newest and cutest girl on her small college campus. When she shared her testimony with her college friends about how she, as a young girl, had miraculously escaped the Nazis, everyone admired and loved her, as well as her story of courage. She was an instant favorite on campus with her foreign accent, natural beauty, and musical talents. All the guys wanted her attention, and all the girls wanted to be her friend.

Lance, the handsome president of the student body, took note of her popularity and moved in on her. He would not let any other guys get close to her. Faith did not mind. She was naive and unfamiliar with American ways. Even her father, who was still learning English, was impressed with Lance. He had no objections when Lance asked Faith to be his wife.

The wedding was beautiful. After the ceremony, however, her world crumbled.

On their way to the hotel, her new husband suddenly changed. "Don't talk to me," he said. "I don't want to hear your voice. I can't stand your accent."

Lance dropped Faith off at the hotel, leaving her alone on their honeymoon night. She never learned where he went. When they moved into their house and finally had sexual relations, he treated her with contempt. During sex, he would say, "Turn this way, now flip that way." There was no love. What was she to do?

One day, while at home, she sang and played worship songs on the piano. Without warning, Lance snuck up behind her and smashed his fist into her head, knocking her unconscious. When she came to, she was in incredible pain. He was holding her, sobbing and promising, "I'm so sorry! I will never do that again! Please forgive me!" Being a good "Christian wife," Faith forgave him because he seemed sincere.

That's why it was such a shock when, months later, she was happily singing and playing the piano when Lance came up behind her and unexpectedly stuck her again. He completely knocked her off the piano stool, and she crumpled to the floor. This time when she regained consciousness, Lance was gone. And this time, Faith was pregnant and lying in a pool of blood.

As she staggered around the house, holding her bleeding head, she found Lance calmly sitting on the couch, drinking a beer, and watching TV. "Why did you hit me?" she screamed.

"It was your fault," he replied with nonchalance. "You were mocking me by playing those church songs."

These incidents continued, and Faith became a regular in the emergency room at local hospitals. Her excuses for her injuries ranged from "I fell down the stairs" to "a hammer fell off a ladder and hit me in the face."

To make matters worse, their house had a basement with a padlocked door, which was Lance's private domain. He had expressly declared it off-limits to Faith. One day, while her husband was away on a trip, Faith was determined to break into the forbidden room.

When she finally opened the door and turned on the light, she was horrified. Pornography covered the walls. Magazines, books, sex toys, and movies depicting every perversion imaginable filled the room. Faith could hardly breathe. She quickly relocked the door, promising herself she would never tell a soul.

Lance had been living a lie their entire marriage. For years, Faith hid all these incidents from her son, her parents, her church, and all her friends. The physical and verbal abuse continued for twenty years.

On the day her son left for college, Faith served divorce papers to Lance at his office. When Lance arrived home agitated that evening, he shook the divorce papers in his hand. He angrily told Faith that he always despised her and had never loved her. He disclosed that he'd had sex with multiple male and female partners.

When she finally told her son the truth about his father, her son began to cry and shared his pain as if a dam had broken. He confessed to his mother, "I knew he never loved me, but I just never knew why. I always thought there was something wrong with me!"

Sometime after the honeymoon, when you step down off Cloud Nine, the vampire who charmed and dazzled you at the altar disappears in the mirror right before your eyes. He will turn on you and rip you to shreds when he reappears. In some cases, this happens immediately after the reception; in others, it occurs when the first conflict arises.

The lovely compliments vanish. Instead of compliments, you will receive the opposite message of disdain. Suddenly, without warning, you move from "stupendous" to "stupid." Once the verbal abuse begins, physical abuse may not be far behind. A marriage vampire believes and will swear that he will never hurt you again ... until he beats you senseless tomorrow. Eventually, he will deny that he ever hit you in the first place.

Billy and Sheila

When they married, Sheila was a twenty-year-old college student, and Billy worked in the family's self-storage business, where he ran one of the large units. He had been a handsome and dashing high school athlete but had never done well in school and had no interest in college. Billy lived in a house on his parents' property and was their "platinum" child. They adored him. No matter what happened, there was always a way to explain away any incident or problem. Nothing was ever Billy's fault.

Billy wanted to have sex on their first date, but Sheila, raised with Christian values, refused. From that time on, he was determined to have her. He told her he loved her and wanted to get married right away. He was so persistent she finally agreed to marry him. What could possibly go wrong?

After they married, they moved into a house Billy's parents had built for them, next to theirs. Sheila just knew it was going to be fantastic. But Sheila quickly discovered that her and Billy's ideas about marriage were quite different.

Billy's focus was always on sex. Early in their marriage, he walked around the house naked, wanting Sheila to do the same.

Sheila was uncomfortable and embarrassed. "Oh, don't be such a prude," he would say.

She eventually agreed to comply in the privacy of their home if the shades and curtains were closed. But his voyeurism didn't stop there.

Next, Billy wanted to take nude pictures of Sheila, telling her it made him think about her all day while he was at work. She reluctantly agreed to a photo session but later began to fear someone might discover the pictures. She decided she'd never pose nude for him again. He moped around for days, but she stood her ground.

When Sheila came to see me as a client, she and Billy had been married for eleven years and had two children. Billy's mother provided childcare for their children and still considered her son the platinum child.

Sheila, who had a college degree, was employed outside the family business. She was a great employee, received promotions, and was now making more money than she'd ever dreamed.

Billy wasn't as fortunate. After his father died, Billy inherited the storage unit, but the family business was stagnant. As Sheila began to make more money, she wanted to buy a larger home as an investment, but Billy wouldn't agree or even discuss the possibility. He resented her success, and he was frequently critical and constantly angry about trivial problems at work. He spent his time in his office, watching porn and wasting time.

Sheila went to prepare breakfast one morning, only to discover that, inside the refrigerator, a large, nude picture of Billy was propped against the milk carton. She was aghast and did not think having the photo on view was funny. She asked him, "What if the children had seen this?"

"Oh, that?" he said. "It's no big deal. C'mon, honey. I just wanted to give you a little hint of what you can expect later tonight. Thought I would take some pictures of you, too."

Sheila was stunned. "Billy, I thought you were past all that," she said. "We're not high school kids anymore. I manage over two hundred employees. I don't need nude pictures of myself floating around." Billy was sullen and angry, but they did not discuss it again.

This was when Sheila decided they needed marriage counseling. Billy refused. She came alone to my office to seek direction. Before the next counseling session, Billy staged a romantic evening and sent the kids to his mother's house. There were flowers and a candlelight dinner. Billy explained he was trying to make up for being insensitive about the nude photos and told Sheila he was turning over a new leaf.

After dinner, when they went to bed and started to become intimate, Sheila noticed that Billy kept attempting to position them toward a specific spot on the bed and realized something was wrong. She got up, walked over to the closet, and discovered a hidden video camera, recording everything.

Sheila was enraged. She knocked the camera off its tripod, smashing it into pieces.

She quickly dressed and went next door to get the children. She brought them home and slept in their room. Sheila told Billy she couldn't live with his behavior and asked him to move out the following day.

Suddenly, Billy was very willing to attend marriage counseling, but Sheila was finished with him. Billy's mother thought Sheila was being too dramatic, so Sheila decided to put the children in daycare, far away from her husband's bizarre antics and his approving mother's control.

From that moment on, Billy and his mother conspired against Sheila. They explained to her that the house was, in fact, the mother's property. Sheila would be forced to move out of her home if she didn't return the two children to her mother-in-law's care.

Sheila couldn't believe her ears, but she refused to accept their demands. Sheila immediately took the children, moved into a rental house, and refused to talk to Billy until he had a psychological evaluation. Because of his behavior, she wanted to ensure the children would be safe with him. His mom insisted Billy go to court to get full custody of the children and offered to provide the funds for a trial.

Billy had another idea. He employed three young men who hung around nearby storage units to abduct his wife from her new home, drive her to a secluded area, and kill her.

The three men almost reached their goal. They attacked Sheila and managed to kidnap her and her children. But when they attempted to slash Sheila's throat, they missed the artery. Sheila lay bleeding in the back seat of their car as her abductors headed for a place to drop her body.

She reacted intelligently and kept her cool while also keeping her terrified children as calm as possible. She promised her kidnappers not to tell anyone about what they had done if they would simply take her and the children home. When the panicking hired hands saw the amount of blood pouring from Sheila's neck, they lost their nerve, drove her and her children to her house, and sped away.

Sheila immediately called 911 and was quickly transported to the hospital. Her children were placed in protective custody. The police quickly apprehended the would-be killers, who confessed that Billy had paid them to kill his wife. Billy was arrested and jailed.

As you may imagine, things did not go too well for Billy as the case proceeded. He had always been rescued when he was in trouble before, but the platinum child would tarnish this time. Billy is currently serving time in prison for attempted murder.

Sheila, now afraid for her life, gave up her career, changed her name, distanced herself from her own family, and moved to another state. I imagine she is still picking up the pieces. Billy's mom patiently waits for her platinum child, whom she believes was "framed," to come home. I never heard from Sheila again.

As a family therapist, I have observed that many victims I counsel are incredibly strong people. They have been carrying their family on their backs for years. They are the ones who take care of things at home, especially the children. They must be the steady, dependable parent, while the marriage vampire is out impressing others and desperately trying to convince them he is successful.

Sheila was a strong woman who refused to crumble due to Billy's charades. She held her ground and almost died because of it. This was a dramatic situation. If Sheila had seen the early warning signs, she could have avoided misery and the tough decisions she later was forced to make to ensure her and her children's safety.

Darrell and Nancy

Nancy, a well-educated, articulate woman, a stay-at-home mother of two, was married to a remarkably successful medical professional. She called my staff for an emergency appointment. When she entered my office, and the door closed, she burst into tears as she tried to tell me her story.

She had received a call from her doctor's office the day before our counseling session, asking her to make an appointment as quickly as possible. When she arrived at his office, her doctor immediately shared the results of her recent tests.

Her physician said, "I received the results of your biopsy, and unfortunately, it shows you have stage 2 cancer. We want to schedule surgery immediately, followed by treatments to destroy all other cancer cells that may be present. I have to warn you that there are no guarantees that this treatment will work."

Nancy was utterly devastated, and everything went into slow motion. She could not even respond. The doctor saw her shock and said, "You will need your husband's complete support. We want to schedule an appointment for both of you to come in together. I'll help in any way possible."

Nancy picked up her cell phone to call her husband, Darrell, but he did not answer. Nancy then called his secretary but was told he was too busy to talk to her. Nancy told the secretary it was imperative—an emergency. The secretary relayed the message, but as usual, Darrell disregarded it. He always discouraged Nancy from contacting him at work.

Nancy somehow had the stamina to drive to Darrell's office but could not speak when she saw him. She simply handed him the test results.

When Darrell read the news, he was furious. "What am I supposed to do if you die?" he asked.

Nancy could not believe what she was hearing. It got worse. He started yelling at her as if the cancer were her fault. "You picked a fine time to complicate my life!" he yelled.

As calmly as she could, Nancy said, "The doctor wants to talk to both of us. He said I'd need your full support during this crisis."

Darrell exploded. "Who is going to take care of the children? How am I supposed to get my job done now? Just get out of my office! I need to be alone so that I can figure this thing out!"

Nancy ran out in tears, and that is when she called my office for an emergency appointment. It finally dawned on her that Darrell did not care anything about her. If she died, he would get someone else to care for the kids. He did not say, "Honey, together we're going to beat this," or, "We will ask God for a miracle." No, he was more concerned about how her condition would affect him

Because of his self-centered view of the world, a marriage vampire only sees his own needs. Everyone he allows into his circle should consider themselves privileged.

If you see this trait in a potential husband, RUN! If you are already married to a marriage vampire, let me help you understand something: Do not take it personally. You did not cause his disorder—and you cannot cure it.

Nancy was facing cancer and possible death, and all her husband could see was a childcare problem. Nancy saw her marriage and her husband's character clearly for the first time. She had been living in a one-sided relationship the entire time. It was like she had been picked from a mail-order magazine to fit into his portfolio. Darrell had no compassion for her at all. His complete lack of empathy alarmed Nancy more than her disease, which she did beat—on her own.

After seeing his response, Nancy left Darrell to begin a new, much happier life.

Charles and Cathy

Although Cathy's husband, Charles, had always been arrogant and could be controlling, she never thought of him as all that bad. His behavior begged to differ.

Once, Charles was almost arrested when tickets he wanted for a specific event sold out. After attempting to charm the ticket agent at the window—even offering a bribe—he went berserk when he could not buy any tickets. Charles would throw a tantrum in any restaurant that wouldn't immediately satisfy his demands, leading waiters to defer to him rather than allow him to cause a scene. On occasions, however, he would become so loud that he would be instructed to leave, sometimes under police escort.

Cathy thought she and Charles got along well most of the time. If he got mad, he tended to pout, which she didn't particularly feel as threatening. She knew he would never apologize for anything, and nothing was ever his fault, but she had decided to accept this and live with it. Cathy enjoyed high self-esteem, didn't feel endangered by Charles, yet would become annoyed. Her parents had a loud, abusive, chaotic relationship, so in comparison, her life was not so bad, even though she and Charles were not emotionally close.

And then her life made a turn. After years of being in a one-sided relationship emotionally, she met a man who was as strong as Charles had initially appeared to be. This man's strength and confidence were no act, and she was attracted to him immediately. Cathy began to spend more time with him and would try to find reasons for them to be together. They never did anything physically inappropriate, but she began to confide her feelings to him. She felt she could talk to him about anything.

Eventually, Charles heard a rumor that the two were having an affair. Even though there had been no physical contact of any kind, she admitted to her husband that she had felt strong feelings for this other man. Charles went off the deep end, but he became the suffering martyr rather than becoming aggressive. He behaved as if he were the victim. How could she do this to him? He pointed out that an emotional affair was even worse than a sexual affair, and he said he wasn't sure he could ever recover from such betrayal.

Charles demanded that Cathy never see her friend again and discontinue activities outside the home to prove she was sorry for what she'd done. From that day on, he supervised her schedule, questioned how she spent her time, and forced her to prove she was faithful. His idea of penance meant Cathy must do things in the bedroom she had always refused to do in the past. He said she had to make up for the pain she had caused him.

Because of Charles' behavior toward her and his demands upon her, Cathy's life became a constant reminder of the sin she felt she had committed. She had been separated from family or friends who might have supported her. Eventually, she began to wonder about the sexual behavior he demanded. Where did all these strange ideas come from, and why did she have to degrade herself in this way—bondage, dirty talk, and calling herself names? Where did he come up with this stuff?

She stopped wondering when her doctor told her she had Herpes, a sexually transmitted disease (STD) that can last a lifetime. What?! Charles was the only man she had ever been with physically, and she knew one did not get STDs from commode seats. When she confronted her husband, he denied transmitting it to her. He called her a whore, saying she had slept with the other man. But this time, his accusations wouldn't work. She knew the truth and was not going to back down. "No! I got this from you!" she said.

For the first time, Charles became physically violent. He grabbed her arms and slammed her against the wall. "How dare you question me after what you've done!" he yelled. "If you ever tell anyone about this, I'll tell the world about your little affair!" He threatened to beat her, left the house in a rage, and didn't return for two days.

During that time, however, Cathy got busy. First, she called the police to report the assault. She then went through all his credit card bills and check stubs. Cathy found receipts for hotel rooms, gifts, flowers, and jewelry purchases that she'd never received. When Charles finally arrived back at the house, he was arrested for domestic violence, served with a protective order, and taken to jail. He told everyone he knew about her affair, conveniently forgetting to mention he had been visiting prostitutes during the marriage and that he was addicted to pornography.

To his surprise, his friends did not feel sorry for him. They did not believe that emotional affairs were worse than sexual affairs—or giving your wife a lifetime STD. Upon notification of his "unjust" arrest, his office manager accessed his work computer and found it filled with porn. Unceremoniously, Charles was fired from his job.

The last time I spoke with Cathy, she was in the process of obtaining a divorce and moving closer to those in her family from whom she would receive more support.

A marriage vampire believes that he is in control. He should not have to wait his turn in line, park in the back of the lot, or yield to oncoming traffic. He assumes he deserves preferential treatment and expects others to do as he asks. They must always agree with his view and value him as the expert on everything.

If you fail to meet his expectations, a marriage vampire will perceive that you are the one who should be "fixed," not that his view of things or his behavior should change. This guy needs to be the boss, not the hired help, the hammer, or the nail. He believes he has been elected king of the planet, and all others should bow to his demands. His authority is not to be questioned at all.

Jim and Laura

After the death of Laura's first husband, she was lonely and missed being part of a couple. She had loved her husband very much, but he died after a lengthy illness. She missed not being able to do things they had enjoyed doing together. After a few years, she decided to begin to date again. She was determined only to date Christian men who were either widowed or had experienced a "scriptural" divorce. She wanted them to be financially stable, not smoke, drink, or watch porn.

Laura thought she had hit the jackpot when she met Jim, the president and founder of a small missionary training school. Jim's wife had died years earlier, and following her death, he had poured himself into his work. He was tall and handsome, with silver hair and a great speaking voice. He preached at a church he began on the campus of his school. He had traveled on missions around the world and spoke five languages. He acted charming, knew the Bible well, and had a good singing voice. He was outgoing, dynamic, and an influential fundraiser.

Jim asked Laura to come to his next fundraising event. Since Laura loved dressing up for special occasions, and after years of isolation, she was thrilled to have opportunities to become socially active again.

After a brief courtship, they were married at his church. The place was packed. The couple honeymooned around the world, with Jim taking her to visit his former students who were now missionaries. Laura saw things she never dreamed she would see. When they returned, she moved into his house on the school campus. This would become her new home.

Soon, however, she learned Jim had a foreign female "assistant," who had served as housekeeper and host for his social events before their marriage. This assistant did it all. She shopped, cooked, cleaned, and even did the laundry. She lived on campus and drove the school's vehicle. The woman was from Bangladesh and was incredibly quiet, almost withdrawn in Laura's presence. However, she came alive when Jim walked in the door. Although the woman spoke fluent English, she and Jim only communicated in her native language, even when Laura was present and couldn't understand what was being said.

Over time, as his new wife, Laura expected to assume the tasks the assistant had been performing. The house was small enough for her to manage effectively, and she had enjoyed cooking and taking care of Jim on their honeymoon. She was an excellent cook and host and was an exemplary housekeeper. She was surprised by Jim's desire to keep the assistant around. He explained he was helping the woman by giving her this job and that it was part of his ministry.

Eventually, Laura became more insistent that this employee was not needed in their home, and she wanted her gone. Jim finally acquiesced. Laura was now able to get a little peace as she thought the assistant was no longer involved in their daily lives.

The next surprise was to learn the woman was managing Jim and Laura's finances, as she had when she lived with them, and was, in fact, still paying their bills. She knew all their personal information. Again, this was a task Laura had done for years and had expected to do for Jim, as well. But this is where he drew the line. He was not willing to change "his system," as he called it, because it had worked for him quite well in the past. Laura was free to keep her own money and separate accounts, but Jim would not change his.

Laura began to wonder what this woman did now that she wasn't Jim's housekeeper. Was she working for the school in another position? A quick investigation told her the answer was no, at least not as far as anyone else knew. Laura became increasingly suspicious that this woman was more than an "assistant," and anyone in a position to provide information would suddenly clam up when asked. They all encouraged Laura to ask Jim directly about "that."

Soon, Laura began to spy on Jim and discovered he would visit this woman's house from time to time when he was supposed to be preparing a sermon or studying for a class. When she finally confronted Jim, he became angry and refused to discuss the issue. She found herself served with divorce papers the very next day, along with a generous settlement that would be hers if she signed a provision that she would never talk about the marriage.

She later learned from a school employee, who swore her to secrecy, that when her husband's first wife fell ill, the relationship with the Bangladeshi woman appeared to take on new dimensions. He began to have sex with this woman and continued that relationship after his wife's death. He only married Laura after people started to talk that he and his assistant seemed a little too close. Laura soon realized that she was cunningly courted as a cover for this man's affair.

The whole thing—the courtship, the crooning, the sermons, the wedding vows, the honeymoon, the ministry, and the sweet, modest home on his campus—had been one big, well-orchestrated lie.

Once Laura knew the truth, even though it was bitter to learn, she was free. This marriage vampire had seriously bitten her, but she stood her ground and refused to give him any more of her blood. Jim had proven to Laura that her life was worth nothing more to him than a showpiece. She helped him obtain the right image and the appearance of integrity. As soon as Laura, his "wonderful jewel and precious bride," confronted him, Jim kicked her to the curb.

Rather than clinging to her pride or being swallowed up by shame, Laura chose to follow instructions she found in Ephesians 5:6-13 (RSV). "Let no one deceive you with empty words, for it is because of these things that the wrath of God comes upon the sons of disobedience. Therefore do not associate with them, for once you were darkness, but now you are light in the Lord; walk as children of light (for the fruit of light is found in all that is good and right and true), and try to learn what is pleasing to the Lord. Take no part in the unfruitful works of darkness, but instead expose them. For it is a shame even to speak of the things that they do in secret; but when anything is exposed by light it becomes visible, for anything that becomes visible is light."

If Laura had submitted to Jim for the sake of maintaining a mask of godliness, like others who chose to keep his secrets, she would be living a lie for the rest of her life.

Instead, she decided to wear the "mark" of a Christian divorcee and she disclosed what had happened in their marriage.

Laura knew that she would only find peace once she was free of this marriage vampire and had exposed what he had done, even though others at the university and church knew (or suspected) what Jim had been doing for years but hid their knowledge to 'protect' the institutions. By their actions, they had allowed Jim to continue his behaviors, which had ensnared Laura, and deceived others.

She decided to choose peace over a dysfunctional life with this vampire. Laura left Jim.

As with many vampires, Jim quickly regrouped to pull his defenses around himself, disappeared from her life, and, in his mind, he emerged from this confrontation unscathed. He lied about Laura, and those people charmed by him and his charisma, especially those within his atmosphere, chose to believe him.

Laura lost friends at the university, as some didn't believe the truths exposed during the divorce or still chose to support Jim. But Laura knew the truth and had done what she knew was the right thing to do.

Laura returned to her former life, surrounded herself with Christians whose beliefs were rock-solid, and escaped the lies of a narcissist who would have destroyed her life and her faith. Her experiences influenced her to reject anger and bitterness and instead become an inspirational writer and speaker teaching women about marriage, true Godliness, faith & trust in God.

3

Revealing His Lies

"A lying tongue hates its victims, a
flattering mouth works ruin."
(Proverbs 26:28, RSV)

I do my best to support women who find themselves entangled in a marriage vampire's disordered world. To him, you are whatever he says you are—whether it is intelligent, dumb, perfect, or disgusting. To win every argument, the marriage vampire will say whatever he wants to say and be as vicious as he wants to be. If you try to defuse the situation by agreeing with him or attempt to appease his lies for a relative semblance of peace, that is all narcissists will need to declare victory. "I told you so, didn't I? You're hopeless!"

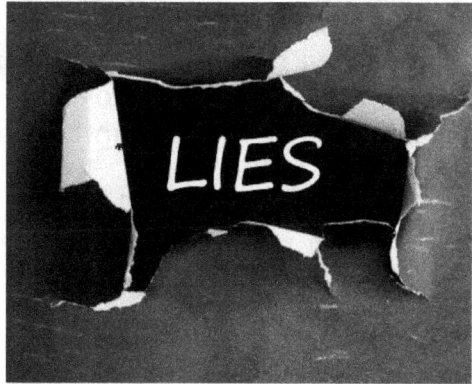

Before you know it, you are spinning down the rabbit hole, leading to endless recycling of his double talk, until you start to believe everything he has said about you. As his long days of berating turn into weeks, months, and even years, you slowly realize that you are no longer relevant to your marriage or the marriage vampire, and if you don't do something about it, no one will.

In his eyes, you are nothing but an object. Your value to him is whatever he decides it is (and is subject to change without notice). Do not take it personally.

Not a Normal Situation

In a Christian marriage, a bride promises certain things to her husband-to-be because she believes in a mutual covenant that reflects Christ and His bride, the church. Ordinary people are bound by their word. Marriage vampires are not bound by their word. Contracts are supposed to bind two parties, not one.

Now, this is where his disorder goes to another level.

The marriage vampire has every intention of doing what he promised at the altar; he meant every word. The only problem is that he may not hang onto his promises past the parking lot. He will flip his opinion of you. You never know when it will happen. But when the marriage vampire decides you have no worth to him, he will believe that with equal sincerity and intensity.

Ordinary people do not switch between love and hate, yet marriage vampires do this easily.

"For that person must not suppose that a double-minded man, unstable in all his ways, will receive anything from the Lord." (James 1:7-8, RSV)

A marriage vampire will mask the truth by vehemently denying he is ever wrong, lacking, or guilty of anything. Of course, he is lying. But he will never admit he is lying.

"If we say we have no sin, we deceive ourselves, and the truth is not in us." (1 John 1:8, RSV)

If the marriage vampire has no truth in him, what does he have? Lies! He redefines the marriage vows to meet his plan, enslaving you for his desires and benefits. He will constantly build webs of deceit and lies designed to keep you in a state of confusion. And when his web entangles you, he will slowly drain your life right out of you.

Why does he do this? *Because that is who he is.* There is no truth in him. I will repeat this over and over throughout this book. You must grasp this fact if you are going to defend yourself.

The first key in unmasking the vampire is to know the truth about him. He has a disorder, and what he is doing is not normal behavior.

Those who have been under a marriage vampire's spell for a long time, like Linda, can barely lift their heads. They have been in this battle for so long they cannot recognize the truth. But when the truth finally dawns on them, these broken women are astonished. "You mean I'm okay?" they ask. "Are you telling me that this is not my fault? Are you telling me that I am not the problem? Are you saying he is the problem? Are you saying all those things he told me were lies?"

"Yes, yes, yes, and yes!" I tell them emphatically. "You've got it! Now, hold onto it."

Oh, sure, you have made mistakes, but *you* are not a mistake. You have had failures, but *you* are not a failure. And yes, you have been fooled, but *you* are not a fool. The one attempting to devour you has pierced you with these derogatory labels, like arrows from a bow. As you begin to understand the truth, you will be able to remove these arrows, one by one.

Are You Ready for the Truth?

Truth is truth, whether we believe it or not. Two plus two equals four. It does not matter who says it; that is the truth. Everything God says is true. When God says, He "sits above the circle of the earth...," in Isaiah 40:22, RSV, that is also the truth.

In the seventeenth century, everyone believed the sun revolved around the earth and that the earth was flat, not round. Then along came Galileo, who proved the earth revolved around the sun. The leadership of the day said to him, "We're going to kill you if you say that!"

"Wait! Never mind! You're right!" Galileo exclaimed. "The sun does revolve around the earth, and I don't need to die."

God's truth remains steadfast and is always God's truth. Will you believe His truth about you?

As a counselor, I explain to my clients that God's Word is like a healing ointment. It is time to immerse yourself in God's truths because they will change your thinking. Listen to the loving things God says about you:

"He [the Lord] raises the poor from the dust and lifts the needy from the ash heap." (Psalms 113:7, RSV)

"But you are a chosen race, a royal priesthood, a holy nation, God's own people, that you may declare the wonderful deeds of him who called you out of darkness into his marvelous light." (1 Peter 2:9, RSV)

"...and her who was not beloved I will call 'my beloved.'" (Romans 9:25, RSV)

"But because of his great love for us, God, who is rich in mercy, made us alive with Christ." (Ephesians 2:4, NIV)

"I love those who love me, and those who seek me diligently find me." (Proverbs 8:17, RSV)

Even though you may feel that you have lost so much—your name, property, inheritance, position, value, honor, voice, dreams, place, future, your security—the truth is, you have never, ever, lost them in God's eyes. The enemy's words may have buried these truths, but they are still there. God has always considered you (past, present, and future) of the highest value, a precious treasure.

God has set your value. You are not your own. You have been bought with a price, and that price was the blood of His son. He gave everything for you. That is how deeply He loves you. He holds you in the highest esteem, valuable like rubies and diamonds and so precious He gave his son for you.

In contrast, what does Satan want to do with you? He wants to steal you from God and trample you under his feet. Satan's goal is to destroy you.

Are you valuable? Yes!

"You have searched me, Lord, and you know me." ..."I praise you because I am fearfully and wonderfully made;" ..."How precious to me are your thoughts, God! How vast is the sum of them! Were I to count them, they would out-number the grains of sand..." (Psalms 139:1, 14, 17-18, NIV)

God thinks about you all the time. You cannot even begin to comprehend His thoughts of you. The next time you are walking along a beach, try to count the individual grains of sand on the shore, some as fine as powdered sugar! When God thinks of you, He does not add up your sins and calculate your transgressions. That is what Satan does.

Before Peter denied Christ, Jesus told Peter:

"...Satan demanded to have you, that he might sift you like wheat, but I have prayed for you that your faith may not fail..." (Luke 22:31-32, RSV)

Satan would not accuse Peter of something that Peter would not do. Instead, Satan was accusing Peter of some-thing Peter was about to do! Satan does not need to lie about us. He can tell the truth about us and our sins. We all sin and make mistakes, so we give Satan all the ammunition he needs. But Jesus goes to His Father on our behalf, knowing we will sin, and intercedes for us. Jesus didn't forgive Peter because Jesus never condemned him in the first place. He loved him even when He knew Peter was about to betray Him. Jesus loves us with that same intensity.

However, the marriage vampire will do everything he can to convince you that you are unlovable.

That is a lie!

The word "unlovable" does not exist in God's kingdom, just like the word "condemnation" does not exist in God's kingdom.

"There is therefore now no condemnation to those who are in Christ Jesus." (Romans 8:1, RSV)

Why? Because it is the truth! You no longer suffer the abuse and debasement of Satan's lies, designed to discourage and judge you, no matter from whose mouth they come.

Let's do an exercise. Insert your name in the following verses where prompted:

"For God so loved <YOUR NAME> that He gave His only Son, that <YOUR NAME> who believes in Him, should not perish but have eternal life." (John 3:16, RSV)

Remember what Jesus said: "The thief comes only to steal and kill and destroy; I came that <YOUR NAME> may have life and have it abundantly." (John 10:10, RSV)

With His gentle words, God wants you to understand that He has already built a firm foundation under your feet for you to live an abundant life. He will whisper the truth into your ears about who you are and fill you with all His strength. He will protect you from the plans, the lies, and the destructive ways of any marriage vampire. God does not want you to be anxious. He does not want you to worry. Why? Because you are already in His hands.

"He who dwells in the shelter of the Most High, who abides in the shadow of the Almighty, will say to the Lord, 'My refuge and my fortress; my God, in whom I trust.' For he will deliver you from the snare of the fowler and from the deadly pestilence; he will cover you with his pinions, and under his wings, you will find refuge; his faithfulness is a shield and buckler. You will not fear the terror of the night, nor the arrow that flies by day..." (Psalms 91:1-5, RSV)

Your True Identity

You must know God loves you constantly! He loves you, even when you make mistakes every day.

"The steadfast love of the Lord never ceases; his mercies never come to an end; they are new every morning; great is your faithfulness." (Lamentations 3:22-23, ESV).

God wants you to know this today and tomorrow. He wants you to feel secure and brave, love yourself, and stand up to anyone who tries to steal your sense of worth. In Romans 8, Paul tells us that God the Father, God the Son, and God the Holy Spirit are rooting for you!

"For you did not receive the spirit of slavery to fall back into fear, but you have received the spirit of sonship. When we cry, 'Abba! Father!' it is the Spirit himself bearing witness with our spirit that we are children of God..." (Romans 8:15-16, RSV)

We would worry about productivity if we worked on a family farm and were servants or slaves. If servants, we might be fired. If slaves, we might be beaten or sold. But what if we were children of the owner? We would one day inherit the farm!

We are neither servants nor slaves. *We are sons and daughters of the Most High God.* He has adopted us as His children, and we will one day be glorified with Christ.

His Spirit bears witness with our spirit that we are children of God. We do not have to be afraid that someone will take that relationship away from us anymore. As if that were not enough, to assure us that He is on our side, the Holy Spirit will intercede for us with sighs too deep for words, according to the will of God, and will witness to God that we are His children.

All our life, we've believed the lies that we must be perfect, and we must work hard to be pleasing to God. Those lies are Satan's attempts to make us doubt the immense value God places on us, rather than believing God when He says we are precious to Him.

"If God is for us, who can be against us? Who will bring any charge against those whom God has chosen? ... Christ Jesus who died – more than that, who was raised to life – is at the right hand of God and is also interceding for us." (Romans 8:31, 33-34, NIV)

Where I grew up, when you broke the law, if your father was the judge and your brother was the district attorney, you wouldn't be charged with a crime. It's not about nepotism and a broken system (although there's that); it's that the judge and D.A. love you and don't want to see you condemned.

God doesn't condemn you either. God did not look the other way. Instead, He sent His son to die for our sins. There is never any indication that God will stop loving you.

In the following passage, He lists every possibility: "Who shall separate us from the love of Christ? Shall tribulation, or distress, or persecution, or famine, or nakedness, or peril, or sword? As it is written, 'For your sake we are killed all day long; we are accounted as sheep for the slaughter.'

Yet, in all these things, we are more than conquerors through Him who loved us." (Romans 8:35-37, NIV)

"For I am convinced that neither death nor life, neither angels nor demons, neither the present nor the future, nor any powers, neither height nor depth, nor anything else in all creation, will be able to separate us from the love of God that is in Christ Jesus our Lord." (Romans 8:38-39, NIV)

An abusive marriage is not a sign that God has stopped loving you. It is not a sign that God has condemned you. A critical, controlling, hurtful marriage vampire cannot come between you and the love of God. But that doesn't mean Satan will stop accusing you or trying to convince you otherwise.

"Then I heard a loud voice in heaven say: 'Now have come the salvation and the power and the kingdom of our God, and the authority of his Messiah. For the accuser of our brothers and sisters, who accuses them before our God day and night, has been hurled down." (Revelation 12:10, NIV)

Remember, you are God's child. You are completely loved and completely forgiven, and if you believe in Jesus Christ as your Lord and Savior, you will live forever in His presence.

Now that you know who you are, and who the real enemy is, you understand that Satan is at war with you. His perversion of marriage is designed to turn you into his slave. He wants you to think that being married to a marriage vampire is normal. However, you are *not* in a typical marriage. The marriage vampire has only one goal: to serve himself by subjugating you.

He has been doing an excellent job of deceiving you. But now, you can reclaim your life, breathe a little deeper, stand a little taller, and heave a sigh of relief.

4

Love and Marriage

"Do not throw your pearls to pigs."
(Matthew 7:6, NIV)

Lyricist Sammy Cahn had it right when he penned the song "Love and Marriage," first made famous in 1955 by Frank Sinatra. Love and marriage are inseparable. "You can't have one without the other." To believe anything else is an illusion.

What Is Love?

Throughout the centuries, the definition of the word love has morphed into something quite different from God's intent. Love has become common and sometimes even crass. We love ice cream; we love a walk on the beach; we love the latest nail color; we love a particular movie, a great song, a poster, a cupcake, and our pet iguana. What kind of love are we talking about?

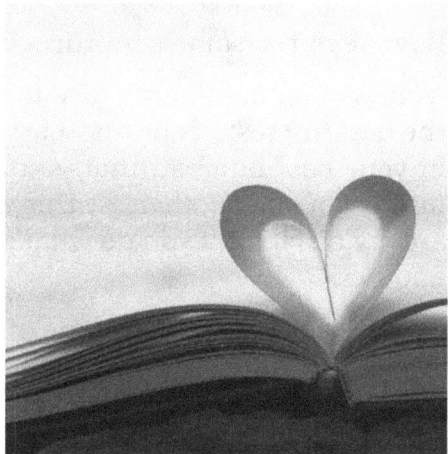

The definition of love God speaks of is often buried and forgotten. Our culture has taken love, the essential element for a full life, and watered it down. The true definition must be resurrected and restored to its proper place.

Ancient Greeks had four words for various kinds of love we can experience:

Phileo: Brotherly love or fellowship.

Eros: Romantic or sexual love.

Storge: Familial love or natural affection.

Agape: Doing what is in the best interest of others. God uses the same word for love.

If your marriage begins with agape love, it can carry you through your entire life. All the other types of love spawn from this one; agape love never dies. God says to "Love your enemies" and to "Love your neighbor the same as [you love] yourself," (Matthew 5:44, NIV; Mark 12:31, AMPC).

Agape love is required for you to live your life to its fullest potential. "A new commandment I give to you, that you love one another; even as I have loved you, that you also love one another. By this all men will know that you are my disciples, if you have love for one another." (John 13:34-35, RSV)

Now, read the same scripture, but with love defined:

"A new commandment I give to you, that you do what's in the best interest of one another; even as I have done what's in your best interest, that you also do what's in the best interest of one another. By this, all men will know that you are my disciples if you do what's in the best interest of one another."

Agape love is the cornerstone of a God-designed marriage.

Marriage is the culmination of God's creation.

God declared marriage "good." He designed marriage to eliminate loneliness and create oneness between man and woman. God said, "It is not good that the man should be alone..." (Genesis 2:18, RSV). God gave him Eve. Now Adam was complete in Eve, and Eve was complete in Adam.

This is the unity that God ordained and blessed for our good, and it is the ultimate design of all things created.

Hitting God's Mark in Marriage

In Ephesians, the Apostle Paul sets the mark for marriage when he instructs us that "Husbands, love your wives, as Christ loved the church and gave himself up for her, that he might sanctify her, having cleansed her by the washing of water with the word, that he might present the church to himself in splendor, without spot or wrinkle or any such thing, that she might be holy and without blemish. Even so husbands should love their wives as their own bodies. He who loves his wife loves himself. For no man ever hates his own flesh, but nourishes and cherishes it, as Christ does the church, because we are members of his body. 'For this reason a man shall leave his father and mother and be joined to his wife, and the two shall become one flesh.' This mystery is a profound one, and I am saying that it refers to Christ and the church; however, let each one of you love his wife as himself, and let the wife see that she respects her husband." (Ephesians 5:25-33, RSV)

In the Bible, the word "sin" is an archery term. It means "missing the bullseye." There is only one bullseye when you have a target, and it's at the center. Hitting anything outside that bullseye is "missing the mark."

People, especially in the church, may say, "Divorce is a sin." Well, duh! So is anything outside of God's design.

The Bible tells us that we *all* have sinned and fallen short of the glory of God. We have *all* missed the mark, and none of us shot too high. That is why Christ came and died for us. He restored us to Him and each other—so we could *hit* the mark.

We have just read about God's standard for our marriages. It may seem a tall order, but He would not have set it up that way or asked us to live it if He had not given us the ability.

God's target for leadership is paradoxical. The leader should be doing everything they can in the follower's interest. That is our model as Christians. A husband who does not lead by serving, who will not give up everything for his wife, who does not nurture and cherish her, is not hitting "the mark." That is what sin means—missing the mark, the bull's eye, the goal, the ideal. God would not tell us to do something we cannot do. What kind of love are we talking about here? In I Corinthians 13:4-8, we're given a description of God's agape love.

- Love is patient.
- Love is kind.
- Love does not envy.
- Love does not boast.
- Love is not arrogant or rude.
- Love does not dishonor others.
- Love is not self-centered.
- Love does not insist on having its own way.
- Love is not easily angered.
- Love is not resentful.
- Love is not irritable.
- Love keeps no record of wrongs.
- Love does not delight in evil but rejoices with the truth.

- Love always protects.
- Love always trusts.
- Love always hopes.
- Love always perseveres.
- Love never ends.

A marriage vampire is the opposite of agape love. He has not only missed the target, but he never showed up for target practice. He is envious, boastful, and proud; he dishonors you and others; he is self-seeking, easily angered, keeps a record of wrongs, and delights in evil; he believes his lies, exposes your personhood and says you're hopeless. He has given up and always seems to fail you.

Is this the covenant you signed up for? I don't think so. What kind of marriage were you hoping for—to love and be loved? Well, yes.

God's Marriage Plan

To understand God's plan for marriage, it is vital to know what role both the man and woman play within marriage. Let's look more closely as the apostle Paul outlines God's plan in the Book of Ephesians, stating that the husband should love (do what was in the best interest of) his wife as Christ loved (did what was in the best interest of) the church and gave up everything for her.

As a husband, it is my role to give up whatever I must do to meet my wife's needs. Christ gave up his place in heaven and gave his life for his "bride" (the church). What should I give up for my wife? Whatever it takes: time, money, hobbies, friends, family, career, or any other interest.

Now, strangely enough, the plan does not say, "Wives love your husbands." Instead, wives are to submit to their husbands as to the Lord by appreciating and respecting them.

"Wives, submit yourselves to your own husbands as you do to the Lord" and "...the wife must respect her husband." (Ephesians 5:22; 33, ESV)

Let me explain my view of that verse. To me, that verse means to respect and follow the leadership of a person that God has instructed to lead in a loving and caring manner, just as Christ does for his bride, the church.

You can read the Bible all day long, and you will not find God telling husbands to be critical, demanding, or harsh with their wives. It is just not God's pattern. If a man is not the kind of leader God says he should be, can he have the kind of marriage God wants him to have? The answer is simple: No.

Every time Christ tells someone to follow a leader, He first lectures the leader. In the following example, Jesus' disciples argued about their position in God's kingdom. Who was going to oversee the others?

Jesus used every opportunity available to teach his disciples. He said that in his organization, the church, the leaders served the followers. This teaching was a surprising concept to them.

"Jesus called them [the apostles] together and said, 'You know that the rulers of the Gentiles lord it over them, and their high officials exercise authority over them. Not so with you. Instead, whoever wants to become great among you must be your servant, and whoever wants to be first must be your slave—.'" (Matthew 20:25-27, NIV)

"After that, he [Jesus] poured water into a basin and began to wash his disciples' feet, drying them with the towel that was wrapped around Him... 'Do you understand what I have done for you?' He asked them. 'You call me "Teacher" and "Lord," and rightly so, for that is what I am. Now that I, your Lord and Teacher, have washed your feet, you also should wash one another's feet. I have set you an example that you should do as I have done for you.'" (John 13:5, 12-15, NIV)

The husband leads by doing what is in the best interest of his bride. God instructs the man to be prepared to accept his wife and family's financial, emotional, and spiritual responsibilities. Ask single moms you know, and many may tell you that they would be happy to have a loving partner in their lives who would help them.

God does not command all people to be married. He does, however, have a "mark" (goal) for those in a marriage. People can make it on their own, but "two are better than one" simply because they can provide added support for each other.

When we go back to God's manual, we read, "For the husband is the head of the wife as Christ is the head of the church..." (Ephesians 5:23, RSV).

What does "head of the wife" mean? It is *not* a lordship over someone. It's the very opposite! It is being a *servant*.

The Wrong Kind of Submission

I have heard hundreds of horror stories over the years about "Christian" husbands using Ephesians 5:22-24 to dominate or browbeat their wives into submission. *This is not God's will!* Selfish men have taken these scriptures entirely out of context. A man who does not have the Spirit of God in him cannot understand that his position, as a husband, is to bless his wife, not to attack or harm her.

It is a rare passage where the name of our loving Lord and the word "hate" appear in the same verse. It does not get more severe than this:

"The fear of the Lord is hatred of evil. Pride and arrogance and the way of evil and perverted speech I hate." (Proverbs 8:13, RSV)

The narcissist thinks, "God says I am the head of my wife. I do not plan to give up anything for her. She must give up everything for me and submit to my authority!" He will say to his wife, "The Bible says that I'm the head over you. That means you must do whatever I say."

It appears that some Christian husbands have forgotten they are to be following God. Every action Christ took on Earth was for His betrothed—to prove His love, His healing, His teaching, and His promises. When Jesus knew He would endure beatings, be held in disdain, disrespected, spit upon, publicly ridiculed, abandoned, and finally killed, He continued in pursuit of His bride—the church. Christ willingly gave His life to set her free from the bondage of this world.

If that is our example, the marriage vampire certainly is missing something here. *How could anyone twist the scriptures by saying the husband's job is to place his wife back under the very bondage from which Jesus saved her?* That is only something Satan would do. The bride agreed to submit to her husband as the husband was under submission to God. *That* is the husband God says you should follow.

Remember the example Paul gave to help a husband understand the profound significance of his role: "Husbands, love your wives, as Christ loved the church and gave himself up for her" (Ephesians 5:25, RSV)

The husband is to provide for and protect his wife. As he does, she, in turn, recognizes he does so out of his love and care for her. He wants her to feel secure. He wants her to feel safe. He wants her to feel loved. The husband is to live considerately with his wife.

For example, if a husband and wife were sitting on the couch watching TV, and he felt cold, he could say to her, "I'm going to grab a blanket—would you like one, too? Do you want to share a blanket?" If he were thirsty, he could ask her if she also would like something to drink.

The Perversion of Marriage

The spouse of a marriage vampire does not live in the marriage described in the Bible by Peter and Paul. She lives in the oppressive, critical, painful bondage brought about by the marriage vampire's selfishness and his inability to understand the needs of others. He has perverted the Word of God and has convinced his Christian spouse she is under obligation to endure whatever he dishes out. Then he tells her to submit to his selfish demands, and any refusal means she does not please God because she does not please him.

Because of this perversion of God's truth, wives may be subjected to inappropriate behaviors or demands from the marriage vampire. Instead of giving their wives strength, marriage vampires burden their wives with demands.

This is *not* the marriage God designed. It is clear the kind of marriage He tells us to stay in, and although He does not tell us what marriage to leave, notice the statement at the end of the quote: "Wives, submit to your own husbands, as to the Lord." If your husband is a drug dealer, a kidnapper, a robber, a pornographer, etc., should you follow him into ungodliness? No!

"...do not throw your pearls to pigs. If you do, they may trample them under their feet, and turn and tear you to pieces." (Matthew 7:6, NIV)

This was Jesus, a Jew, talking to a Jewish audience. Jewish people who keep kosher do not raise pigs or eat them. They consider pigs unclean garbage eaters that eat, drink, and live in filth. By using this analogy, Jesus taught us not to give something highly valued and precious to a creature who does not value it. You don't put a diamond wedding ring on the hoof of a wild pig!

The marriage vampire will step on your values and then turn and tear you to pieces. Jesus does not say to kill the wild pig or to hate the wild pig. He tells us to quit giving the wild pig our precious things.

You are priceless. You must stop throwing yourself down in the marriage vampire's muddy pigpen, believing you will be cherished. It is just not in him. If these men did not

63

do so much damage to their wives, I would feel sorry for them. What does God say you are supposed to do?

"Run for dear life from evil; hold on for dear life to good." (Romans 12:9-10, MSG).

"Let love be genuine; hate what is evil, hold fast to what is good." (Romans 12:9, RSV)

"Do not be wise in your own eyes; fear the Lord and shun evil. This will bring health to your body and nourishment to your bones." (Proverbs 3:7-8, RSV)

The faithful Christian husband has a Bible verse to live by and a warning if he does not.

"Likewise, husbands, live with your wives in an understanding way, showing honor to the woman as the weaker vessel, since they are heirs with you of the grace of life, *so that your prayers may not be hindered.*" (1 Peter 3:7, ESV)

In the days of Christ, people used pottery for cooking. These pots were virtually unbreakable and could be tossed around with little care. The Egyptians, however, made beautiful, hand-painted pottery as thin as an eggshell. This pottery was intricate, fragile, expensive, and used as decoration.

People may have expensive crystal stemware received as a wedding gift. We wouldn't let a three-year-old play with our stemware, we do not throw it in the dishwasher, and we do not store it with our Bama jelly glasses. We display the stemware in a fancy cabinet and treat it as precious.

Your husband is to treat you as if you are precious, like this crystal stemware. He is living with God's daughter, with whom he is a joint heir as children of God. That is why God gets involved.

It is essential to understand that God sees wives as precious and extremely valuable. That does *not* mean women are weak!

Think of a Faberge egg, covered in jewels, each is one-of-a-kind, and each contains a surprise. A Faberge egg was one of the most valued gifts given by Russian royalty. If a man treats his wife as if she is the most precious thing in his eyes, how would she respond?

A marriage vampire perceives himself as royalty and the rest of us as commoners. A man may be God's son, but a woman is God's daughter. God is highly interested in how she is treated. If a husband does not live considerately with God's daughter, God will not listen to that man's prayers. Those prayers will be hindered. If a man wants God's favor, he will treat God's daughter as if she were precious.

Living with agape love toward one's wife—considering their needs—means a wise husband would:

- Provide for his wife (financially create stability and security for her)
- Protect his wife (both physically and if attacked emotionally)
- Nurture his wife (things she needs to grow or flourish)
- Cherish his wife (value and love her)
- Be gentle (compassionate) to his wife

Men try to love and cherish their wives, but a marriage vampire cannot do it. He sees no value in other people—including you. He cannot nurture and cherish you because he has no empathy.

Because your marriage vampire has stolen part of who you are, you will have to stand and reclaim your worth. As you find yourself at a crossroads of knowing the truth, you will have to prepare yourself for the battle to come.

"For freedom, Christ has set us free. Stand firm, therefore, and do not submit again to a yoke of slavery." (Galatians 5:1, RSV)

5

Combating Constant Lies

"You honor me with your lips
but your heart is far from me."
(Matthew 15:8, RSV)

You have read how a marriage vampire can wreak havoc in a relationship. You may have experienced it firsthand.

Marriage vampires are afflicted with a unique disorder and are experts at manipulation. A vampire can turn on a dime when attempting to obtain what he wants. He may appear sincere, but there is no truth in him. He has been perfecting his persona—his shell—his entire life. He believes every lie he tells is the truth.

How Marriage Vampires Protect Themselves

Marriage vampires have incredibly thick shells, like an oyster, with layer upon layer of ego defenses. Ego defenses are not lies we tell—they are lies we *believe*. Inside an oyster's shell, however, an oyster is entirely defenseless. No claws, no teeth, no skin. They are exposed and completely vulnerable.

Marriage vampires spend their entire lives attempting to protect themselves from this vulnerability, building layer upon layer of ego defenses over time that becomes more and more rigid until the lies become their identity, even though they remain weak and defenseless inside. They believe their thick shells protect them and prevent others from realizing how fragile they are.

I'll share specific examples of the shells and layers (ego defenses) that marriage vampires create for protection.

EGO DEFENSES

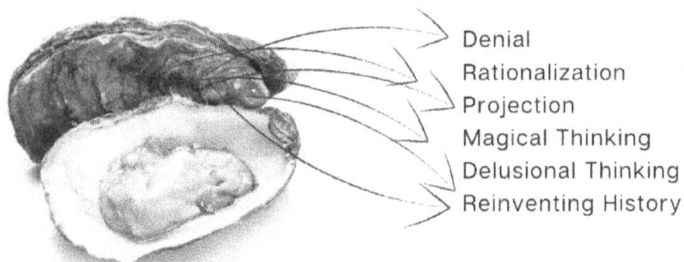

Denial
Rationalization
Projection
Magical Thinking
Delusional Thinking
Reinventing History

Ego Defenses

The ego is a person's conscious sense of personal identity or self. Defenses are safety measures a person uses to protect oneself from perceived threats, whether the threats are real or imagined.

Ego Defenses include denial and rationalization, projection, magical thinking, delusional thinking, and reinventing history. I will discuss each of these ego defenses below to clarify how a narcissist thinks.

Denial and Rationalization

Denial is a primitive ego defense. Even young children will use it. It is the easiest shell to detect.

Denial is the ability to believe things did not happen the way they did—and to go as far as to claim what happened did not happen. Such as:

- "I didn't say that."
- "I didn't hit you."
- "I didn't call you that name."
- "I didn't go there. You're lying."

Rationalization is a little more elaborate, but not much.

Rationalization is claiming a positive or benevolent reason a thing happened the way it did. Such as:

- "I told you that so you wouldn't worry."
- "I was going to do what we planned, but a better deal came along."
- "I didn't mean to do that, but because it worked out, it didn't hurt anything. It was okay."
- "I had to talk to her again. I didn't tell you because I knew you'd get mad and think I was trying to get involved with her again."

Projection

Projection is a complex ego defense. It is the ability to project your attitudes, beliefs, and emotions onto others. Vampires believe they can "read minds," so to speak. They think they can tell you what you think, feel, and believe. They appear so certain of your motives; they might convince you to doubt yourself.

Projection is how vampires see you as *all good* (when attracted to you) and see you as *all bad* (when angry with you). By projecting their bad feelings on you, they can then rationalize almost any behavior they choose.

"I did that because I know you're cheating on me, and I wanted you to know just how bad it feels inside."

"You did that just to hurt me."

"You don't believe that. You are saying that to make me look bad."

"You're so selfish. All you do is think about yourself."

When a vampire is angry with you, he believes you are angry with him. When he is no longer angry with you, he thinks you should no longer be angry with him. You should instead be pleasant. He is surprised that you are still hurting from what he said or did, and he will "act as if" nothing ever happened. "Why are you holding this grudge? That's not a Christian thing to do."

Magical Thinking

Narcissists can dream up a scheme, then believe that whatever they do, no matter how badly they act, they will get away with it. They will make insane decisions and be amazed when they do not work out. These decisions may be about money, his career, or his relationship with you. This type of thinking allows the vampire to do anything and believe things will be okay, even though they may do something as dangerous as drive while drunk or invest your life savings on a "tip."

One man bought his and her Jaguar sports cars because he thought they were a great buy and that he would be able to pay for them somehow.

Another vampire, fired from his job, decided not to tell his wife, or change his spending habits because he believed he would get an excellent job soon. He did all of this while spending time hanging out in strip clubs and pretending to be at work. His wife did not know what he was doing until they received a foreclosure notice at their door.

A vampire will engage in affairs believing no one will ever find out. Oh, the delusional web he weaves! His magical thinking assumes the other woman will keep her mouth shut and the other woman's husband will not find out and call the vampire's wife.

The terrifying aspect of the marriage vampire's magical thinking is that he believes something will save him. This allows him to try anything he wants. He expects his magical ability will help him land on his feet, or he can use his smooth-talking skills to talk his way out of things, believing he can escape or make natural consequences disappear.

Magical thinking pairs with projection. You can hear him now: "It wasn't sexual harassment! They had it in for me because I was making them look stupid. None of the women I work with would dare say anything about me unless they were pressured into it."

If caught, they will get away with it; if charged, they will beat the rap; and if arrested, they will explain that it was all a big misunderstanding and nothing to worry about. When wives try to confront vampires with their magical thinking, vampires will attack them for lack of faith or being negative for no reason. They refuse to change their ways. One husband of a client is sitting in prison right now. He would not take a plea deal because his magical thinking determined that the jury would understand his reason for embezzling funds at work.

Delusional Thinking

When you believe a lie, you are delusional. When you think you can leap tall buildings with a single bound, you are delusional and believe a lie. Delusional thinking allows the vampire to believe he can never be wrong, never suffer a defeat, that no failure is his fault, and to think he can somehow get out of any situation he is in.

Marriage vampires believe they are of more value than the rest of us, which explains their arrogant and demanding behavior. They don't think they'll ever be caught because they consider themselves more intelligent and more cunning than everyone else.

Our culture is partly to blame, as we worship success and see influential people get off the hook all the time. We tell people to "look out for number one" and "see you at the top." These vampires tend to count their chickens before they hatch and see themselves as winning the game in the first quarter. We fall for their scams and Ponzi schemes. We cannot wait to hear their success stories because we want to win, too! But trust me. Vampires are not winners. They may get ahead because they sell out or give up everything to get what they want. But they are never happy or fulfilled, and they are always looking for their next conquest.

Another way society contributes to a vampire's delusional thinking is to provide excuses for their behavior and images to project upon the rest of us.

One powerful reinforcer for the marriage vampire's delusional thinking is pornography. Pornography is evil, disgusting, and much more insidious than most people think. Most men run into pornography before becoming an adult. It is common for men to find Christian women who have never seen pornography and do not know much about it. If women do think about pornography, they think of it as "soft-core" porn, the least-offensive type—pictures of women with their clothes off on bearskin rugs in front of fireplaces, back when porn was only pornographic magazines and pin-up calendars.

The computer age changed all that. Now anyone can sit in their house or place of business and tap into the multibillion-dollar network that is extremely happy to provide the vilest images that Satan can inspire. People can purchase porn on cable, satellite, and the Internet, or obtain much of it free. A variety of porn is available and comes from very dark places.

Women, teens, and even children are portrayed in demeaning ways. Pornography presents as normal while containing all kinds of abuse paired with vile sexual behaviors. It is delusional to think mistreatment of another person is normal. It is a federal crime to possess or download child porn to your computer, cell phone, or printer.

There is a worldwide network, mostly from foreign countries, which victimizes children in this way. It is sick. It is evil. It is corrosive. By the time men's secret pornographic addictions are revealed, their wives are shocked at the filth they have been viewing. Porn can be addictive.

"So God let them go. He allowed them to do what their sinful hearts wanted to. He let them commit sexual sins. They made one another's bodies impure by what they did. They chose a lie instead of the truth about God. They worshiped and served created things. They didn't worship the Creator. But he is praised forever. Amen. So God let them continue to have their shameful desires. Their women committed sexual acts that were not natural." (Romans 1:24-26, NIRV)

Pornography has a dangerous effect on the marriage vampire. It often depicts women as sexually submissive and willing to do whatever a man wants, perhaps even enjoying degrading behavior as if it were fun and desirable. Porn convinces vampires that their wives should be up for anything sexually as they see photographs reflected on their screens of aberrant sexual behaviors. Wives need to know that porn films are just that: films. Make-believe. The women never say "No" to anything because they are there to "serve" men's sexual desires.

This objectification of women normalizes the marriage vampire's view of his wife and his belief that he should have the right to make her meet his desires in the same way. Sex becomes a way to subjugate women and put them in their place. If their wives refuse these demands, it is a reason to force them, punish them, or blame them for not being "good" wives. Porn will lead vampires to conclude that what he sees on his screen is normal, and his wife is a prude if she refuses. Marriage vampires may feel free to get their needs met somewhere else if their wives will not do what they want.

When you catch him, the marriage vampire always has an answer. A vampire will tell his wife that he was caught doing something illegal because she was reluctant to participate in his (humiliating) requests in the first place. It may be shocking to realize that the vampire's view of women is corrupted and reinforced by porn's lies. The lies lead to very painful criticism and ridicule of wives, who frequently wonder where their husbands got these ideas? When you smell a rat, look for it. You may find a hidden catalyst for the vampire's behavior. You may find that the trigger is porn.

"But rather I wrote to you not to associate with anyone who bears the name of brother if he is guilty of immorality or greed, or is an idolater, reviler, drunkard, or robber—not even to eat with such a one." (1 Corinthians 5:11, RSV)

Reinventing History

Reinventing history is the most complex and troubling ego defense (shell) that a personality disorder can use. Because a vampire cannot be wrong without feeling completely worthless, they cannot accept reality when things do not go their way. If forced to accept the consequences of their mistakes, they may find themselves suicidal. Their answer is to simply change the past, something you and I cannot do.

Vampires formulate a past that lets them off the hook and negates their immoral behaviors. This is different from rationalization or denial. In this defense, the vampire constructs a false scenario to explain why he is not at fault. He will have to find someone other than himself as being the problem. He will explain that he was not really to blame, often blaming you. The marriage vampire will look you right in the face and claim you did things and said things you did not do or say.

One vampire told his wife, "I was fired because you told me to lie to my boss!" The truth was the complete opposite.

His wife had begged him not to skip work and play golf on the day the business project was due.

If a marriage vampire beats you up, you started it. If they called you a name, that is the name you called them. If they cheated on you, they say it is because you cheated on them, or they become angry because you would not do what they believe you "should have" done as their wife.

I had a client who accidentally discovered a disturbing videotape. The family's routine was for mom to pick the kids up from school, and as she prepared supper, the children watched an educational video and began their homework. As they were putting up their backpacks, mom hit 'replay' on what she thought was a video for her children. But instead, it was a video of her husband and best friend having sex on her living room couch. Fortunately, her kids did not see the tape as they had not yet settled in the TV room.

When the husband arrived home, however, the wife tearfully confronted him. He said that he and her friend had only 'been acting,' were making a videotape to make the friend's husband jealous, and had done nothing wrong. He began acting as if he were the victim of his wife's uncompromising attitudes and said she didn't recognize what a great guy he was for trying to 'help' her friend who was in a troubled marriage. He completely denied that he and her friend had done anything inappropriate, even though his wife held the video evidence in her hand, and he knew what was on the videotape.

That is how crazy things can become when dealing with a narcissist. It is like living in a surreal world—an alternative universe where reality no longer exists.

One woman told me she thought she was crazy because she could no longer recall exactly what had happened. It was not until she sought help from a counselor that she realized her husband had constantly undermined her confidence by persuading her to believe his reinventing of history.

This is "gaslighting." It is manipulating someone mentally by convincing them they cannot believe what they are experiencing or even seeing. The term originates from a 1938 stage play, *Gas Light,* and two subsequent films (1940 and '44) titled *Gaslight,* in which an abusive husband slowly dims the gas lights in his house while pretending he hasn't, to make his wife doubt her perceptions.

The vampire will hold onto his lie until he can swap it for a better lie. You may be stuck listening to stories that never happened, about friends you never knew, and places you never visited. His trick is to take you down the rabbit hole. Do not go along with his lies! Do not accept his lies, or one day he will use them against you in an attempt to prove your instability. Your trick is to hold on to the truth—for your sanity. The truth will set you free.

Marriage vampires use these same ego defenses on you. You may feel like you are in a trance when attempting to confront them. They have been practicing these ego defense techniques for years and are highly skilled at using them. This is the way they live their lives. It is an incredibly destructive behavior projected onto everyone they encounter, especially their spouses. The truth is, they want you locked up with them in their self-made prison with no way of escape.

I am here to try to show you the way to open the door to the life God promised you—a way out of the marriage vampire's prison, forever.

Do not give in to the temptation to "just leave it." Problems never resolve if ignored. He may stop talking, but you will never convince him that your way is better.

Levels of Communication

There are three levels of communication;
1. The **Issue Level**,
2. The **Personal Level** and
3. The **Relationship Level**.

When we communicate, we are *constantly* communicating on one of those three communication levels. *The only level you can resolve conflict on is the issue level.* Once you leave the issue level, you may as well stop talking. Moving to the other levels only escalates the conflict and draws attention away from the actual root problem.

Three Levels of Communication

Relationship: "If-Then"
"If-Then" statements threaten the relationship STOP

Personal: "You" statements
"You" statements attack the other person. CAUTION

Issue Level: "I" statements
"I" statements stay on the issue.
ONLY level where conflict is resolved! BEST

Copy this graphic to save for easy reference. It can serve as a quick reminder of the effective way to manage conflict.

Issue Level

Issues are anything we choose to discuss, characterized by "I" statements. Examples of these statements might include: "What I want," "What I believe," "What I will do," "What I feel," and "What I won't do."

Even if we communicate on the issue level, it does not mean we *agree* on the issues. You may want to go to the movies, and I may not. When we conflict on the issue level, it may take the form of a debate. You win a debate based on the merits. You persuade your partner that your position is more effective, or your partner convinces you. Even if you disagree, you attack the *issue*, not the *person*.

Remaining on the issue level, while also setting boundaries (which we'll discuss in Chapter 7) might sound something like this: "I will no longer tolerate infidelity in this marriage." "I expect you to be home before 7 p.m." "I want you to help the children with their homework and show interest in their activities." "I will manage my weight." People often, unfortunately, are unable to stay on the issue level for a prolonged period. When conflict or disagreement arises, they quickly jump to the personal level and attack.

Personal Level

Personal-level communication is characterized by "You" statements, which attack the other person and do not address the issue.

"You always," "You never," "You are stupid," "You are crazy," "You don't understand," or other all-or-none statements are the type of statements used in personal level communications.

There are two types of personal-level communication: "Fight Talk" and "Spite Talk."

Fight talk is, "I hate you. I'm going to hurt you."

Spite talk would be, "Poor me. I never get to do what I want."

"Poor me" means "bad you."

Personal level conflict is like boxing; I win when you can no longer answer the bell. I win when you give up or admit defeat. On this level, the meanest, most vicious person wins. The goal is to move the other person off the issue and win by intimidation.

Relationship Level

When you move to this level, it threatens the entire relationship. It is coercive and characterized by "If-then" remarks and ultimatums. "If you do that again, I will leave you." "If you don't stop, I'll never talk to you again." "If you do that one more time, I'll divorce you." "If you don't do what I want, I'll beat you."

People often jump to this level if the other person doesn't give in to them on the personal level. *You cannot resolve any conflict once you leave the issue level.* That is why it is so vital that you remain there.

"Get Out of Jail Free" Card

I will give you a "get out of jail free" card called *"God's truth."* It is the only way to win the battle against the marriage vampire. You will be fighting a well-entrenched, well-trained adversary. With this card, the marriage vampire will no longer be able to disarm you, sweep you off your feet, or pull you into his web of lies. With God's truth, the marriage vampire's game is over.

Remember when you first confronted him, caught him in a lie, or saw him doing something that needed addressing? He deflected all attempts to penetrate his perfect persona (shell). Why did he go nuts on you? To you, this may have been a minor event, but to him, it was life or death. Why didn't he confess wrong or offer to change? Instead, he had to maintain his delusion of perfection at any cost.

Other marriage vampires may have episodes when, under intense confrontation, they may break down. They weep, they wish they could die, they say such things as "Now everyone will know I'm an idiot! Everyone will know what I did. No one will ever love me. They'll all hate me!" For a while, they even believe it.

When a vampire's wife sees this, she usually thinks, "Oh, wow! He gets it! Now we are finally getting somewhere. He is sorry."

You may be surprised when the marriage vampire suddenly reconsiders his statement and quickly repairs this breach in his shell. "I've been thinking about that, and it wasn't my fault, after all."

Now you are back to square one.

Here is another example: "I think we're finally communicating again," you might say. "I'm glad you apologized to me yesterday. That meant a lot to me."

"What apology?" he asks.

"When you said you were sorry," you reply.

"I don't know what you're talking about," he says. "I didn't do anything wrong."

Remember that this is his disorder, not yours. This is his prison, not yours. You did not put him in it, and you cannot get him out. It is rare for a person with NPD to change. I am not here to get your marriage vampire to change his view of himself. I am here to help you understand what you may be living with and help you deal with it.

His tirades and abuses will continue, but you can prevent him from hurting you by having the necessary information, the truth, and the ability to counteract the effects of his behavior. Now that you are aware of the marriage vampire's ego defenses, I would like to share biblical concepts the marriage vampire does not want you to know; empowering tools that every Christian woman has at her disposal, but of which she may be unaware.

A Wise Woman

What if I assured you that you could break down enemy strongholds, repel fiery darts, fend off the vampire's bite, and regain the ground the marriage vampire had claimed as his own? You are not a character in one of *The Lord of the Rings* films, nor are you Joan of Arc. You are playing yourself in the real world in which you live. Should you choose to accept it, your role is to take captive every worldly thought against you and lock it up forever. That's right: You can take every memory of ill will, slanderous backbiting, and damaging statements made against you, lock them in a box, throw it into the sea, and never think of it again. And if you follow God's directives, you will be able to take back what the enemy has stolen!

"For I will restore health to you, and your wounds I will heal, says the Lord, because they have called you an out-cast..." (Jeremiah 30:17, RSV)

If you want to reclaim your life from the marriage vampire's death grip, you must become educated and learn to recognize, understand, and predict his patterns and tactics. It will take the following:

- Knowledge that you are in a real battle.
- Preparation to stand in the next conflict.
- Practice using spiritual discernment.
- Patience! It took a while to get into this situation, and it will take time to get out.

When you know about what is happening to you, you will no longer wonder if you are going nuts. It is not you. Now that you know where the painful darts are coming from, I will show you how to block the marriage vampire from wounding you.

God offers you His protection plan. He covers you so that as the fiery darts head your way, they will fall like harm-less cotton balls at your feet. Are you ready to find out how this works?

You are a forgiven child of the King! And you have armor at your disposal.

6

God's Armor

God has given you powerful spiritual weapons to stop the fiery darts of abuse launched against you. The apostle Paul explains that we do not struggle against flesh and blood, but instead, we fight against principalities and powers in high places. That is Bible talk for Satan. Satan is the father of lies, and all his lies are like fiery darts. It does not matter from whose mouth the lies come. They are Satan's way of demoralizing us to the point that we wonder if God does care about us or could love us. God continues to reassure us that when we have His truth in us, we can withstand all the attacks of the wicked one.

Paul was in prison multiple times for preaching the truth—the good news, the gospel. Roman soldiers guarded him. This would have given him time to become familiar with their armor. He learned to understand the function of each piece. In the Book of Ephesians, he used this analogy to help us visualize who we are in Christ and how to dress each day. God wants us always prepared for the real battle—spiritual warfare—by dressing in His armor.

He has shown us the armor to wear and the order in which we are to put these on to prepare for battle:

"Therefore take up the *whole armor of God*, that you may be able to withstand in the evil day, and having done all, to stand. Stand therefore, having *girded your waist with truth*, having put on the *breastplate of righteousness*, and having *shod your feet with the preparation of the gospel of peace*; above all, taking the *shield of faith with which you will be able to quench all the fiery darts of the wicked one*. And take the *helmet of salvation, and the sword of the Spirit, which is the word of God*," (Ephesians 6:13-17, NKJV)

Familiarize yourself with each piece of armor so you can use it effectively before you engage in a conflict.

The Belt of Truth

When dressing for battle with the marriage vampire, we begin with the *belt of truth, which is the truth of who you are according to God's Word*. This is not a belt to hold up your pants ... this is a WWF wrestling belt! It protects your stomach (gut). A soldier must first defend his stomach from the daggers of the enemy in close-order fighting.

Satan tries to get close and then, out of nowhere, jabs you in the gut when you least expect it. That is why God gives you such a large, thick belt. Now you are ready for thrusts and low blows that, in the past, would have taken the wind right out of you. Before you had this belt, you would have been unable to breathe as the marriage vampire's blows would have poured down upon you like an angry avalanche. With this belt of truth attached, a marriage vampire's attacks do not affect you, and your breathing is uninterrupted.

With this belt of truth, you are no longer afraid. Your marriage vampire wants you to be afraid—of him. Know the truth about yourself. What does the scripture say?

"The Lord is my shepherd; there is nothing I lack." (Psalms 23:1, NABRE)

When you were scared in the past, you may have felt a knot in your stomach. Now that knot is gone, and you are no longer afraid of the marriage vampire—and he will notice this immediately and try to attack another vulnerable area. But you will be ready. This leather girdle will keep fear at bay and give you peace.

This is God's peace that passes all understanding. Your marriage vampire will become puzzled because his blows are not affecting you as they did in the past.

You now know the truth. Keep this piece of armor belted tightly around your stomach.

All people fear rejection and failure. A vampire will play on these natural fears. He will try to convince you that you could never make it without him and that you will have to stay entirely under his control. But if you do, you will become a second-class citizen in your own home. You must hang on to the truth that you are proficient, "...equipped for every good work." (2 Timothy 3:17, RSV)

To strengthen the belt, you must read the Bible or listen to an audio recording of it as often as possible. The more truth you know, the stronger the belt. The more truth you know, the more it stops lies from sticking to you. It is like a Teflon®-treated pan: nothing sticks, and it is easy to clean off with the water of His Word. When you know the truth, a marriage vampire's half-baked lies slide right off.

The Breastplate of Righteousness

When the marriage vampire discovers you're no longer flinching at his below-the-belt punches, he will try to pierce another precious organ: your heart. He does this by saying things such as, "You're unlovable. There is no way God could love you!"

85

Do not worry. God has that covered, too! That is why He supplied the following line of protection, the breastplate.

It was the shiniest and most adorned piece of a soldier's armor. The Romans made this piece of armor out of brass, starting at the neck and extending down to the waist, and constructed from two different metal pieces. A soldier wore one piece on the front of his body, while the other piece protected the soldier's back. Brass rings joined the two parts, covering and protecting the top of the shoulders. The breastplate deflected the enemies' blows and was used in offensive tactics.

The devil will assault your heart. He will tell you that you are not righteous and of no value. The word devil describes "the one who strikes again and again." He is constantly attempting to penetrate your heart with slanderous accusations. If he wounds your heart, you will more likely surrender and give in to him. He targets anyone who stands against him or is in his way. But God calls us to "Stand!"

You may say to yourself, "I am not righteous." That is true, as "...all have sinned and fall short of the glory of God..." (Romans 3:23, RSV)

That includes you, and that includes me, and that includes vampires. We cannot do it by ourselves. We need everything God supplies. This breastplate of righteousness is not *your* righteousness. It is Christ's. He saved you.

"He saved us, not because of righteous things we had done, but because of his mercy. He saved us through the washing of rebirth and renewal by the Holy Spirit." (Titus 3:5, NIV)

The breastplate of righteousness protects your heart.

Remember what 2 Corinthians 5:21 says:

"For our sake He [God] made Him [Christ] to be sin who knew no sin, so that in Him [Christ] we might become the righteousness of God." (2 Corinthians 5:21, RSV)

Christ took all your sins and exchanged them for His breastplate of righteousness, which covers your body and is designed specifically to protect your heart. Even if your heart condemns you, Christ is greater than your heart. Nothing can separate you from Christ's love.

The breastplate is the brightest battle armament in your arsenal, made of pure light. It is the brilliant, blinding reflection of God, the essence of Christ's glory.

"He is the reflection of God's glory and the exact imprint of God's very being, and he sustains all things by his powerful word. When he had made purification for sins, he sat down at the right hand of the Majesty on high," (Hebrews 1:3, NRSV)

Darkness extinguishes in the presence of this light. This brilliant piece of armor reflects His sacrifice for you. Always remember that you're forgiven, never facing condemnation again. Because of Christ, you can stand against the wiles of the devil.

When believers understand that they are righteous due to Christ, and Christ's breastplate is firmly in place, it doesn't matter the number, or the frequency, of the darts the enemy throws at them. None will penetrate. The darts disappear before they even get close to the breastplate. Not one word of condemnation, not one accusation, not one feeling of guilt will touch you when you are wearing His breastplate.

The Shoes of Peace

Our goal is to pursue God's peace. That's not the type of peace you may try to maintain to avoid trouble, where you submit to avoid being miserable or afraid. No, *we are to pursue God's peace by combating fear, condemnation, and anger.*

The Roman soldiers' combat footwear was designed with hazardous spikes, or cleats, which were one to three inches long. These spikes helped the soldier move forward in battle and keep his footing—a stable placing of his feet to hold his ground.

You are given the ability—and the right—to stand your ground and hold onto the peace God has given you.

"For you were called to freedom, brethren; only do not use your freedom as an opportunity for the flesh, but through love be servants of one another." (Galatians 5:13, RSV)

Peace is the result of resting in a relationship with God. It is a tranquil state that comes from seeking after God. When a person has peace, they become filled with calm, inner stability, even during circumstances that would typically be traumatic or upsetting. *The Shoes of Peace allow you to stand your ground.*

Consider the story told in Mark 4 when Jesus was sleeping peacefully in a boat. He was with His disciples when a sudden and terrible storm arose. His followers focused on the storm's violence and reacted franticly. They forgot the obvious: Jesus was right there with them. Jesus, understanding their fear, simply stood against the violence of the storm and spoke these words: "Peace, be still." Christ spoke peace into being. The storm immediately stopped, and the raging tempest calmed. (Mark 4:35-40, RSV)

You can do the same with the fear and the raging emotions within you. Christ has given you that power.

Peace, however, is not necessarily the absence of conflict; instead, it is your knowledge that God is with you, no matter what battle you encounter. The foundation of peace must be so secure and firm that you can move in utmost confidence, with firm footing, unaffected by what you see or hear. This aggressive peace puts you in a position to face any challenge. You will be enabled to stand your ground instead of crouching down in fear.

With the "gospel of peace," in word and action, you have the needed equipment to take back the precious things that were stolen. When you think you cannot go any further, dig in and stand your ground! God wants you to have peace, and these shoes are an armored platform to support you during an attack. Nothing, and no one, can rob you of that peace anymore.

"Now to him who is able to keep you from falling and to present you without blemish before the presence of his glory with rejoicing," (Jude 1: 24, RSV)

"Peace I leave with you; my peace I give you. I do not give to you as the world gives. Do not let your hearts be troubled and do not be afraid." (John 14:27, NIV)

The Shield of Faith

Roman soldiers didn't carry round-shaped shields a la Vikings. Roman shields were like doors, large enough for soldiers to hide behind, about four feet high and two-and-a-half feet wide. Roman shields were constructed of curved, laminated wood, covered with leather, bound with rawhide (or bronze) edges sticking through the wood. The shield was the only moving part of the soldier's armor, designed to protect against flaming arrows, spears, and other various flying objects. You could feel safe behind one of those shields.

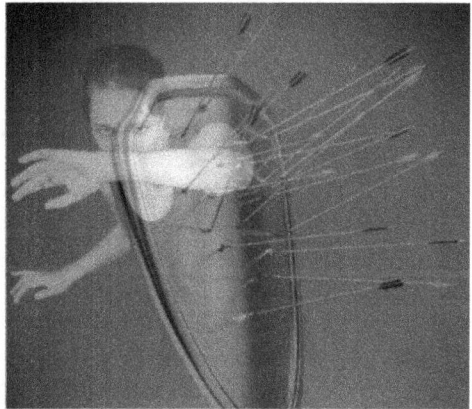

In short, their shields were *big*—and so is yours.

Faith is something like a Roman shield. The Bible gives us a definition of faith in the Book of Hebrews: "Now faith is the assurance of things hoped for, the conviction of things not seen." (Hebrews 11:1, RSV)

To have this kind of faith, you will need to get into shape. There are steps to climb, muscles to exercise, and you will meet resistance. Start at the bottom step and keep moving forward to achieve your goal of victory.

When you are suited up, and fiery darts start to pelt you, and you don't sense immediate results, don't lose heart. Faith is a muscle that should constantly be exercised. Practice makes perfect.

"... this is the victory that overcomes the world, our faith." (1 John 5:4, RSV)

"No, in all these things we are more than conquerors through him who loved us." (Romans 8:37, RSV)

"Therefore, since we are justified by faith, we have peace with God through our Lord Jesus Christ. Through him we have obtained access to this grace in which we stand, and we rejoice in our hope of sharing the glory of God. More than that, we rejoice in our sufferings, knowing that suffering produces endurance, and endurance produces character, and character produces hope..." (Romans 5:1-4, RSV)

Now, when the marriage vampire's lies rage against you, hold up your shield of faith. You are more than a conqueror through Christ Jesus. You can do it! His Word will protect you and is wrapped about you.

This does not mean you won't ever come under attack again, suffer hurt, or never appear to fail.

When Jesus was crucified, it certainly *looked* like He'd failed, but He did *not* remain in the grave.

Christ won over death, and He is sharing His victory with us. Because He won and your faith is in Him, you win, too.

It is not that you "could" or "might" win. Believe in the promises Christ has promised to those who follow Him. You *have* won!

Scripture says that faith is victory over Satan, over a marriage vampire, right here, right now. You are already victorious.

Faith is believing in something and taking steps to accomplish it. God gives us His beautiful blessings of peace, joy, and love. Your faith protects you from those who would try to take it away. You can either trust the shield of faith—the truth God says about you – or you can fear the arrows, i.e., the lies of the marriage vampire. If you believe the truth, you can stand and quench the fiery darts. If you believe the lies, you will continue to be wounded and surrender the ground God gave you. Keep up that shield! *The shield of faith protects you over and over again!*

How will the marriage vampire attack you now that you have armor and protection? He will go for your mind. But God has that covered, too!

Helmet of Salvation

The Bible says, "and you will know the truth, and the truth will make you free." (John 8:32, RSV)

You now know the truth—the truth about who you are in Christ. We are admonished in the book of Romans:

"I appeal to you therefore, brethren, by the mercies of God, to present your bodies as a living sacrifice, holy and acceptable to God, which is your spiritual worship. Do not be conformed to this world but be transformed by the renewal of your mind, that you may prove what is the will of God, what is good and acceptable and perfect." (Romans 12:1-2, RSV)

Are you ready to present yourself? Are you prepared for battle? When the vampire attacks you with lies about your worth, Paul tells us to put on the helmet of salvation. *This helmet protects your thoughts about yourself.* Your spouse may use sarcasm or other critical statements to wound you: "You're not good enough. You never do anything right. You are stupid. You are crazy. No one would ever love you."

But you're prepared. You say to yourself, "Here he goes again." Clink. Clink. Clink. Those arrows hit your helmet and fall at your feet because God has already told you that you are holy—set aside to God—and loved.

We are also told, "Fear not, for I have redeemed you; I have called you by name. You are mine." (Isaiah 43:1, NIV). God knows you personally. He knows your name. He knows everything about you. He has chosen you. He loves you!

Why is the helmet of salvation so important? Because you have been saved, you are not your own; you do not belong to yourself any longer because God bought you with the blood of His Son. That makes you priceless.

The following are examples of lies used to hurt you deeply... as well the truth of what God's Word teaches us about counteracting those lies.

Lie No. 1: "Don't be such a prude!"

In all my years of family counseling, I have only once heard of a narcissist who was not addicted to pornography—and he may have been lying. Pornography breeds all kinds of perversion and abnormal sexual behavior. If people habitually see things, they may become tempted to try those things. A marriage vampire, who is sexually selfish by nature, usually wants his spouse to go along with anything he deems pleasurable or "right," regardless of his partner's comfort level or even the morality of the practice.

If you resist for any reason, the marriage vampire perceives you as trying to deprive or frustrate him. Once again, he will attempt to project onto you. This reduces the most intimate and sacred moments in marriage into degradation and mockery in opposition to what God intended—a precious example of Christ's love for the church. Christ wants your husband to be a blessing to protect you, not abuse or expose you. Physical debasement grieves your spirit and damages your heart. You must protect yourself.

One client shared that her husband suggested, "Anything two married people choose to do together is perfectly OK." She objected to her husband's demands to tie her up like a Thanksgiving turkey. His desires were demeaning, embarrassing, painful, and potentially dangerous. Instead of respecting her concerns, he ridiculed her. If you find yourself in such a situation, avoid such practices at all costs and immediately seek counseling.

Lie No. 2: "You're not pretty enough!"

The marriage vampire is very romantic before marriage, but his rose-colored glasses become misplaced along the path to marital bliss. But remember, this isn't about you; it's about his *perception* of you.

You may find yourself wounded and bleeding from one of his sharp jabs. Do not give up; help is on the way.

If you've been married for a while and he starts complaining about your age, remember that he isn't the young buck he used to be, either. Join the crowd if you are not the size you were on your wedding day. Satan loves to strike at the heart of every woman's self-image. If you listen to his accusations, you will play right into the marriage vampire's hands.

You do not have to listen to his lies. In fact, from now on, listen to the truth about yourself—and the best place to hear it is from God, who cannot lie. The sooner you know that the words coming out of the marriage vampire's mouth are one lie built on another lie, the sooner you will find peace with yourself. This is the first step in your transition to healing. It is not *you*; it is the marriage vampire! Don't be angry with yourself, and don't be angry with him; it's a waste of energy. He has a disorder, and it's not your problem to solve. He is an abuser and can destroy you.

This truth will set you free from his condemnation. Your goal is to obtain knowledge and power to overcome his assaults. Once you can grasp the truth, hang on and never let go.

Marriage vampires are experts at making us doubt. They act so sure of themselves that you may begin to wonder, "Did I ever say that? Did that happen? Am I just imagining that? I must be losing my mind!"

Do not back down from the truth you now know. Truth is truth. It stands on its own. It does not need opinions or debates. It is what it is, and it has the power to set you free.

Every morning, before you walk through the door, put on your helmet and hold your head up high. Let your family and the world know that you are secure in Christ. You no longer live in fear and doubt.

Lie No. 3: "You spend my money faster than I can make it!"

Typically, narcissists love money or the appearance of wealth. If they have not made it financially, they may still buy big hats and drive impressive fancy cars. Vampires have an inevitable attraction to money. They love to throw money and displays of wealth around for others to see.

Most humans have a natural inclination to honor wealth and assume it's the reward of the righteous or that the wealthy are more capable, smarter, or better than others. Not so! Jesus stood that idea on its ear when He confronted a rich, young ruler and told him to give everything he had to the poor, as depicted in Luke 18:18-25, RSV.

The man went away sorrowful, unwilling to part with the appearance of his success.

Those who teach or believe that the financially successful must be close to God have it backward. James taught the kingdom principle of spiritual wealth:

"...Has not God chosen those who are poor in the world to be rich in faith and heirs of the kingdom which he has promised to those who love him?" (James 2:5, RSV)

Believing that rich people are better, or deserve more respect than poor people, is evil.

"Suppose a man comes into your meeting wearing a gold ring and fine clothes, and a poor man in filthy old clothes also comes in. If you show special attention to the man wearing fine clothes and say, 'Here's a good seat for you,' but say to the poor man, 'You stand there' or 'Sit on the floor by my feet,' have you not discriminated among yourselves and become judges with evil thoughts?" (James 2:2-4, NIV)

For a vampire, money is a means of keeping score. If he makes a hefty income, he may believe that entitles him to your worship, and he'll use it to control you. A vampire may give his wife an unrealistically low budget so that she will have to beg for every dollar that she spends.

The Sword of the Spirit

The Roman short sword was known as the sword that conquered the world. This twenty-inch, double-edged sword was short enough to maneuver quickly in either direction, making it both highly effective as either an offensive or defensive weapon. All the other armies had long swords, which were heavy and unwieldy. The Roman sword's design allowed the ability to move and react swiftly, resulting in more victories. *The sword of the Spirit is your weapon, which is The Truth.*

The Romans practiced endlessly with their swords before they went into battle. The sword became an extension of their hands. It could protect them and strike a lethal blow. God wants you trained and prepared before you go into battle so you will know how to manage the truth in every situation.

"For the word of God is living and active and sharper than any two-edged sword, and piercing as far as the division of soul and spirit, of both joints and marrow, and able to judge the thoughts and intentions of the heart." (Hebrews 4:12, NASB-1995)

I find it interesting that the last part of this verse talks about the sword as being a discerner of the thoughts and intents of the heart. Discernment plays an essential role in identifying the ploys of one with NPD.

In my practice, the partners of marriage vampires point out how articulate vampires are and how no one can ever beat them in an argument. No worries. You are not trying to get the vampire to believe the truth; you will tell the truth to yourself—out loud, over, and over:

"I am of value. God says so!"

When we use the sword of the Spirit, we can cut arguments to shreds with the truth and stand against the devil's schemes.

Just as Jesus did in Matthew 4, RSV, you can also tell your attacker the truth. Satan tempted Jesus with food when He was starving, money when He was penniless, and fame when Christ was without friends. All He had to do was give up His mission as the Messiah and His mission to save the abused, lost, and lonely of the world. Satan tempted Jesus by using the Word of God according to Satan's desires and twisted definitions.

Just as Satan used the Word of God to tempt Jesus, your marriage vampire may twist verses from the Bible to use against you. Did the truth change Satan? No. But the sword of the Spirit ripped up every lie Satan threw at Jesus. Satan finally gave up after three tries.

Do Not Give Up! Do Not Give In!

Putting on the whole armor of God empowers you to stand up for yourself and protect yourself from the lies the vampire uses to drain the life out of you. When he throws insults and verbal jabs, you will know he is only trying to manipulate you.

Choose to do whatever *you* want, even if you decide to give in to his demands, not because you are forced to do so, but because you believe it may be the smartest or best thing to do. You do not have to convince the vampire that you are right, and you do not have to make him tell the truth; you can simply do whatever is effective.

I warn my clients that if they decide to defy a vampire, he will try, with even greater intensity, whatever methods he did in the past to convince them to give in. The attacks will become more vicious, determined, and manipulative. There will be more prolonged periods of pouting, whining, and "poor me" ideation.

When a vampire starts attacking or threatening you, there is no reason to continue the conversation, defend yourself, or return his threats. Simply announce what you will or won't do. Even better: do it, or don't do it. This may enrage the marriage vampire; that's nothing new. Stand your ground, take the heat, and let God do the rest.

"It is to one's honor to avoid strife, but every fool is quick to quarrel." (Proverbs 20:3, NIV)

The issue itself is not as important as conveying the reality that you are fully armed with God's protection. You believe what God says about you. You are willing to go toe-to-toe now that you have the equipment and strategy you need for the battle. You cannot overcome evil with evil. You can only overcome evil with good. Never trade insults, threats, or lists of defects with a vampire. Just know the truth and remind yourself repeatedly: "I am holy and loved. I am not condemned." *You* must love *yourself*, and you cannot "win" without getting in touch with God's love for you.

But now, after you have your armor on and your senses about you, the marriage vampire will not understand what happened. You used to give in when he threatened to leave, so now, if you refuse to give in to his demands, he will be forced to back down. If you previously gave in when the vampire threatened to hit you but won't now, he might escalate his threats by striking you.

You must understand: There will be a consequence to your unwillingness to give in to the marriage vampire.

7

Boundaries—and Knowing
When to Leave

*"Be as wise as serpents
and harmless as doves."
(Matthew 10:16, RSV)*

If a country is invaded, its boundaries are breached. The government must then expel the intruder. For example, when Germany invaded France in World War II, France did not say, "Our boundaries have been changed." They said, "We have been invaded!" When the Germans were expelled, the boundaries were reinstated.

Now that you are armored and fighting the good fight, you must first decide your new boundaries. What will and what won't you put up with anymore? Your vampire spouse has proven that you can no longer give him your precious things. Because he does not value you as a treasure, you will have to set boundaries for your protection.

When you decide to create these new boundaries, it won't be like in the movies, where the audience explodes into applause for the underdog. You will be fighting against an adversary who has always subdued you and who believes he can never be wrong. You will have to stop him from crossing your new boundary.

Marriage vampires know no limits. They tend to invade personal space, disregard "No Trespassing" signs, and stake a claim on your very soul, if possible.

Setting emotional boundaries is essential. You may read books or hear advice on television about setting your limits, but it is up to you. Do not worry.

If you set a boundary, you can always move it! You can try out boundaries. If they work for you, keep them. If not, chuck them.

Protect Yourself by Repeatedly Saying "No!"

Decide what you are willing to tolerate. Say no when you get the urge and see what happens. Refuse to go places you don't enjoy—restaurants, parties, and family gatherings.

If he asks you a question in a demeaning tone, don't answer. Refuse to talk to someone who is calling you names or cursing. Don't do things in bed that hurt or are unnatural or make you feel uneasy or bad about yourself. Feel free to protect yourself—morally, emotionally, and physically.

What if you had the right to say "No" simply because you wanted to? What if you had the right to say "No" because you didn't want to do what you were asked to do? Wouldn't that be great?

Well, you *have* that right! Say "No." You have certainly heard it from him repeatedly.

As we discussed, now it's your turn—but be prepared for retaliation. If he calls you names, let him know you will not respond. This is the one thing a narcissist cannot stand—to be ignored. The blood he thirsts for is to provoke a response. If he cannot draw blood, he may pout and leave you alone.

Vampires are, in fact, weaklings. They only feel safe when they control others because they don't trust anyone. They are fundamentally incapable of trust and will want to use control instead. If you give your vampire an inch, he will take a mile. You must be vigilant. If you declare a boundary, keep it. Putting up a "Keep Out" sign instructs people to keep out—whether it is a computer lab or a broom closet.

I have quite a list of arbitrary boundaries for myself— things I don't do because I don't enjoy them, places I don't enjoy going to, types of food I won't eat, actors I don't watch, and games I don't play. These are a part of life, making us more comfortable when we disclose such boundaries.

Others can then choose to respect us or not. If you disrespect my boundary, you suffer the consequences. If you honor my boundary, you communicate that you value my comfort level and respect me.

My father was an alcoholic, so I do not drink. If people offer me a drink, I decline. If they insist, I decline. If they beg, I decline. I decline if they suggest I am stupid or don't know what I am missing. If they disclose that I have hurt their feelings or have insulted them somehow, I continue to decline their alcoholic drink. They can take the first no or the tenth no; it is up to them. But the boundary is up to *me*. They can make me leave, but they cannot make me drink, and they cannot set my boundaries for me.

I have run into people who seem unfamiliar with the word "no." It triggers them. They work hard to try to make me say, "Yes." I occasionally ask, "Is this the first time you've ever heard the word "no?" Do you always get your way?" Of course, they say that they don't *always* get their way—they just get it often. I then suggest they stop looking for a way to manipulate me to give in and use their energy elsewhere.

The Marriage Vampire's Initial Weapon

The question "Why?" is a significant weapon in the vampire's arsenal. "Why did you do that?" "Why did you say that?" "Why did you talk to that person?" Drilling you with this kind of questioning is a form of mental torture meant to confuse you and throw you off guard so that you become defensive and unable to respond effectively.

Who has the right to question you? Teachers question students. Parents question children. Employers question employees. Who has the right to demand answers from another adult?

We give ourselves permission to say "No," as well as decide if a question is fair. We can simply decline to answer if it's unfair or a question we simply don't want to answer. *We* determine if it's a valid request for information—or a means of intimidation, manipulation, punishment, or coercion.

When Christ stood before Pilate, Pilate asked Jesus if he was the king of the Jews. To understand the context of this situation, Pilate was searching for a reason to release Jesus but didn't realize Christ's purpose. Jesus came to this earth to die on the cross for our sins. Pilate was the only one who could put Jesus on the cross; the Jews did not have that power as they were living under Roman domination and control. If Jesus had answered the question truthfully, Pilate would have released him. If Jesus had lied, He would not have died without sin. Jesus decided and chose not to answer, as He fulfilled his purpose. That decision angered Pilate.

In short, if Jesus doesn't have to answer a question, neither do you.

What if a police officer stops you? If you refuse to answer his questions, there will be consequences. If your boss asks you why you were late, and you won't answer, there will be consequences.

Refusing to answer the questions of a narcissist may bring consequences, as well. Be wise about the context.

Perimeter Attacks

We all have boundaries. At some point, we will defend ourselves and push back when marriage vampires try to force us to do things we don't want to do. Sadly, we sometimes allow people to get away with inappropriate behavior because we are caught off guard or don't know how to react. Someone married to a person with NPD may be pressured to do things they never dreamed would be part of a loving and tender marriage relationship.

One client disclosed that her husband would keep arguing his point for hours, no matter what she said. He wouldn't stop pleading, whining, and begging until he wore her down. She would give in to be able to get some sleep. Otherwise, he would keep her up all night.

Name-calling is another way to beat up a person emotionally or psychologically until they surrender. Clients have disclosed to me that these vicious remarks often hurt more than a physical blow, and they tend to heal more slowly.

Fang Marks

Marriage vampires may become physically threatening. They will hit, shake, or manhandle their partners. I always encourage women to report physical abuse to the police. I would never advise anyone to remain in a dangerous situation. As difficult as this may be for the victim, in my counseling experience, I find that once a police officer gets involved, a vampire will often back off or retreat.

When you declare a boundary, the vampire will try his old ways more intensely—all the tricks he knows, repeatedly, hoping you will give in this time. If you collapse from combat fatigue, don't worry. Just get up and start over again. You will have future opportunities to refine your skills and gain victory.

Never Allow Physical Assault

No one has a right to hit you, push you, choke you, or force you to stay in a room or a house that you want to leave. Police label these actions as "assault."

You might be surprised at the control people may suddenly develop in the presence of law enforcement professionals. Setting boundaries may come at a price, but if you decide to stand up, you must stand up all the way.

The law is designed to be on the side of the abuse victim, and if there's an arrest, the abuser may be required to take anger management or domestic violence courses. Most, but not all, vampires will end their behavior rather than go to jail. Others may try to punish their partners for reporting them to the police (but may not show their intent until after the police have left). Again, if physical abuse occurs, you must involve the authorities and refuse to stay in an unsafe environment. Most police departments take domestic violence seriously and do their best to protect the victims.

It's essential to make a distinction between the law and law *enforcement*. Not all police departments or judges are the same. Unfortunately, women in rural jurisdictions and women of color may have vastly different experiences with law enforcement and the judicial system. It is vital to request protection, and if security is not provided, it is crucial to seek other sources or flee immediately.

Because of how narcissists are, they frequently act as if nothing happened after a physical assault. They'll either blame the victim or minimize their inappropriate behavior. The goal is to get him to stop beating you and to start respecting your boundaries, not to get an apology.

Knowing When to Leave

The apostle Paul tells Christians, "No testing has overtaken you that is not common to everyone. God is faithful, and he will not let you be tested beyond your strength, but with the testing he will also provide the way out so that you may be able to endure it." (1 Corinthians 10:13, NRSV)

A woman once told me she couldn't take it anymore. Her marriage vampire had been tying her up for sex ever since their wedding night. This was painful, and she told him so. But he was an expert manipulator. She wore long-sleeved shirts and slacks to cover bruising on her little arms and legs. Her body ached from the physical pain. She would complain, but he would say, "Oh, don't be such a baby!" and, "Whatever we do in our bedroom is OK. It says so in the Bible."

That is *not* in the Bible, but she did not know where to turn. When she said something to his mother, the mother responded, "Now, dear, a wife is supposed to do whatever her husband wants." The wife thought, "His mother is nuts, too. My husband is going to hurt me, and I will not be able to take care of my children."

She gathered all her courage and sternly told her husband that she would no longer allow him to tie her up. As she stood there, feeling strong, he went upstairs to their bedroom, packed his bags, and walked out the door. He never returned. After he left, she found volumes of pictures he had taken of other women he'd also tied up.

She stood her ground and finally controlled her own body again. This guy was twisted. Once challenged, he knew his game was over. He went someplace where no one knew him.

You teach the marriage vampire that his technique works if you give in. If verbal abuse works, it will continue. If hitting works, you will endure the threats of physical abuse until you stand up for yourself or get away from him. That is the only way to be free from his clutches finally. There will be trials. You have already endured troubles and suffering. You have already paid your dues. Now it is time to graduate to a life of hope and promise. How do you do that? One step at a time.

If you stand up to a vampire, things may worsen in the short term. The fights may become longer, the threats bigger, the volume louder. The vampire may lose it. He may forcefully grab you. He may hit you. He may retaliate because you confronted him. He may also pack his bags and leave. Whatever he does, be ready.

Here are tips to consider if the going gets tough:

- Buy pepper spray and keep it handy.
- Stash cash.
- Pack a grab bag with necessities if you must leave in a hurry. (Do not forget an ID!)
- Line up a friend to help you.
- Keep 911 on your speed dial.
- Be prepared!
- Before the next crisis, find out the process of what happens in your town or county when you call 911. (I realize some police departments often do not want to get involved and define domestic calls as the most dangerous. Even if the police do not arrest the marriage vampire, they can take you to a safe place.)
- Go online and find the people/organizations who can help in these situations and make an

emergency list with contact phone numbers and addresses.

- The Domestic Violence hotline can receive texts (text 'start' to 88788) for help. Online & Internet use is impossible to erase completely and can be monitored by a controlling vampire. If this is a concern, contact the Domestic Violence hotline at 800.799.SAFE (7233). Visit their website www.thehotline.org for protection plans, chat, and valuable resources. Be proactive in making a plan that protects you and your family.
- Learn the art of self-defense.
- Seek professional counseling.
- Do not live in fear for your life! Get the help you need to feel safe.

Be smart and consider the consequences. Do not stand up until you are ready. Develop a safety plan and become aware of shelters, churches, or other support systems that assist the victims of aggression. Be prepared to run! You will need an ID, clothes, toilet articles, cash, and other items for an overnight or extended stay in a safe place. The local battered women's shelter can be an excellent resource for what you will need if you must escape. They can help you put an escape plan together and obtain needed legal advice for you and your children.

Exceptions

I'm only aware of two exceptions in the New Testament regarding marriage, and both empower women. Those exceptions are regarding divorce due to infidelity and separation.

The Bible tells us: Don't lie, don't steal, don't kill. It does not say, "Don't lie unless you're scared, don't kill unless you're angry, and don't steal unless you really want that item." It simply says we do not do those things, and it never gives exceptions or allowable permission to do them.

The Bible tells us not to divorce but then provides an exception if infidelity is involved. It tells married couples not to separate but then explains that if you do separate, to remain single.

Separation

Unfortunately, people may remain in life-threatening situations because they don't know their options.

Picture this: A woman rushes to the hospital emergency room to see her severely burned young son. When he finally regains consciousness, she asks, "Why did you stay in the bedroom? Why didn't you run for your life when the fire broke out in the house?" The boy whispers, "You told me to stay in my bedroom." The mom responds, "When I told you that, the house was not on fire."

Learn to protect yourself. You decide your boundaries and what you will say "No" to. You'll find it will be worth it, no matter what happens. You'll feel better about yourself and your future if you set healthy boundaries and enforce them.

Separation is one of the most effective tools clients have found in dealing with vampires. God uses this tool to empower women. Separation can bring about tremendous results, especially with borderline marriage vampires.

God allows you to separate from your husband: "To the married I give this command—not I but the Lord—that the wife should not separate from her husband (but if she does separate, let her remain unmarried or else be reconciled to her husband), and that the husband should not divorce his wife." (1 Corinthians 7:10-11, NRSV)

This forces the narcissist into an exceedingly difficult situation. He cannot make you come back, and if you remain faithful to your vows and he also abides by the principles of separation as laid out in the Bible, he cannot divorce you. This means he will have to negotiate with you. This empowers a woman to escape an unloving, uncaring, abusive husband.

The vampire is forced to make a decision when you are out of the picture. He can lose you, or he must change. Vampires must always be in control. When you walk out the door, he loses his control over you. He is not in charge anymore. If he genuinely can't live without you, this will devastate him, and his shell may break. He may end up crying over the phone, begging you to come home. Remember, now you control and decide how long you need to be gone. You decide when or if you think he has changed. You name your boundaries—what you will or will not allow. Should you return, if he does not live up to your demands, you can always leave again.

The Bible has no limits on the number of times you can separate or for how long. While you are separated, God is able to work on your heart to strengthen you and give you wisdom, but He may also work, through your prayers, on the heart of the vampire.

Protect Yourself at All Costs

Whatever it takes, you must regain control of your own life. Studies show that the average battered wife flees her husband seven times before leaving for good. You may ask, why would she ever go back in the first place? Because an abusive marriage vampire will beg, plead, and promise that it will never happen again if she returns. She believes him, and he never does it again—until the next time.

As women mature, they begin to demand more out of life. They begin to trust their judgment and instincts and realize they can participate in decisions they previously were "too busy"—or didn't have the energy—to make. When these women begin to change the rules, the "fur will fly," Even if it's a good thing eventually, it will trigger conflict with the vampire.

But now you are ready for him. Your armor is in place, your trust is in God, and your confidence is intact. You have a plan. You can look the marriage vampire directly in the eye and say, without raising your voice, "I am no longer going to put up with this behavior." Now stick to it.

Your ultimatum may include parenting issues. You tell your partner you will no longer allow him to hit you, verbally abuse you, or ignore the needs of the children. In most states, laws require reporting suspected child abuse cases to the appropriate agency or facing criminal charges. That law also applies to spouses.

Educate yourself regarding the law, and then tell the vampire what you will and will not tolerate.

Follow up on your threat and report any future abuse to the authorities. Your children only have you to protect them. Interestingly, this is the time most women are willing to report abuse—not to defend themselves but to protect their children.

Divorce

When married to a vampire, if all else fails, leave. I realize that's easier said than done, and for Christians, it is a serious decision.

Divorce is not to be taken lightly, even when a marriage vampire is involved. Differing opinions exist regarding Christians and divorce, and I recommend you both study the Bible and talk to your minister if you are struggling with this decision.

One clear thing is what Jesus said when asked about his position on divorce: He answered that one could divorce for reasons of sexual impurity.

God made us. He knows that if infidelity causes loss of trust in a marriage, the marriage may be broken beyond repair. It may be challenging to live with someone we can no longer trust. Unfaithfulness by a partner strikes at the very core of trust, which is necessary for a loving marriage to thrive.

It may surprise you to learn that most marriages can survive an affair. Two-thirds of marriages in which one partner is unfaithful do make it. In the case of multiple or lengthy affairs, however, it has been my experience that most of those marriages do not survive. Once trust is gone, it is not easy to earn it back.

Think about it: If God commanded us to stay with an unfaithful partner, what would happen after we caught them cheating again? What would life be like when he comes home late, or she gets calls, and the caller hangs up, or the spouse makes the excuse that he forgot his cell phone and that's why he couldn't let you know he would be late getting home? It would be a living nightmare.

Because God made us, He is aware that some people would be unable to live with that betrayal. He makes an exception for infidelity. We have a loving, caring God!

Historically, women (and children) have been considered property rather than people of equal value. Jesus did not see anyone that way and instead considered every person as loved by God.

Jesus once clarified to a group of men that the no-divorce law, except for infidelity, prevented a man from simply divorcing a woman if he grew tired of her, if she made a mistake, did not look right, or didn't do exactly what he wanted. The listeners were surprised that Jesus was telling them they could not simply divorce or discard their wives whenever they wanted.

As we read Matthew 19:10, NRSV, we see that even Christ's disciples were surprised at this new way of viewing women when they said, "If such is the case of a man with his wife, it is better not to marry." Jesus told them it was the right way to consider a marriage partner. When your spouse views people as objects and only cares about himself, you become a thing to be used and discarded, just as those men did in the days of Christ.

What About the Children?

You have a choice whether to go or stay. You will have to determine both the costs and the benefits of your decision. Vampires can be great providers and may diligently try to be remarkably successful. Others are successful in their minds while others are always "about to make it," relying on their partners to bring home the bacon.

Kids are frequently the complicating factor. If you share children with a marriage vampire, the marriage vampire may fight for them, which creates a situation where a spouse may believe the children should have two parents who are together. Occasionally, people love their marriage vampire mates and do not want to leave, knowing the marriage vampire will fall apart or threaten suicide. Even if a spouse does go, when they and the marriage vampire share kids together, they will have to interact with their ex-spouse for the rest of the children's lives.

Women have asked what I believe is best for the children. There is not a single correct answer to that question. Some children may be adaptable and adjust to circumstances, while others cannot manage to do that. Bottom line: You must consider the best scenario for each child. I usually tell moms that they are the "heart" of the family and that if the decision is terrible for her, it is rarely good for the children. Take care of yourself so you can take care of the children.

Children may be targets of marriage vampires, just as are their mothers. In this case, you will have to protect them, too. Kids may also be exempt because they are the marriage vampire's children, but you are not! The cloak of protection may cover the child, but you are fair game. It can become complicated, and there is no correct answer. Consider all the factors.

I have seen a vampire dad, who had little interest in his children, suddenly declare he couldn't live without them. He might put on quite a display in court. He may stay involved—even after the fight is settled. He may transform into the father he had claimed to be.

Most marriage vampires, however, revert to their former monstrous selves. After all the misery they have caused, they simply lose interest and move on with their lives. I have seen vampires manipulate the court and continue to fight for years, right up until the kids became adults.

Consider the monetary issues. Depending on the state in which you live and the state laws, whoever gets custody of the children receives child support.

I knew of a mom who went to work waiting tables to pay court-ordered child support to her doctor husband, who "won" the kids in court. The mother said it was worth whatever it took to regain her life, that she was the best mom she could be, and that she trusted things to work out eventually.

God says it is better to have a crust of bread and peace than it is to be in a house full of feasting, strife and quarreling. (Proverbs 17:1, NCV, NIV).

The issues are determined legally in most cases, but the emotional turmoil continues with no winners, only losers. Many victims tell me it is better to fight at a distance than to fight across the breakfast table. It gets old either way. However, is it easier to hang up the phone or ignore the doorbell to obtain relief?

Couples are never supposed to get back at each other through the children, criticize or attack the other parent, play poor me, or use the children as tools or weapons against the other spouse. Unfortunately, those situations are how most victims are already living. Sometimes the only choice is fighting in the marriage or the divorce court.

The fact is that many women won't have the option to stop fighting with a narcissist. But they *can* learn to fight from a safer distance and with the support and strength they need. The important thing is to stand and fight. Fight for yourself and your children if they are being emotionally or physically harmed.

Mothers have told me that if they divorce the narcissist, they fear their children will be hurt when with their father. That is sad, but it is also life. How much more likely would they be hurt by his influence if they were with him in the same house all the time?

No matter what, be the best mother you can be in whatever situation you find yourself in. You can choose to go or to stay, but you must be sure to remain true to yourself.

If You Decide to Leave

If you are determined to fight, you go to boot camp first. Get in shape, learn the necessary skills, become familiar with the tools, armor, and weapons. Once you are prepared, it's time to join the fight. If you are strong and determined enough, sometimes the other guy gives up.

Think of that. What did our parents tell us to do with bullies? We are taught to stand up to them. I prefer that the ninety-pound weakling work out and kick sand in the bully's face only after he has packed on another ninety pounds, like in the ads in the comic books of my youth. Either way, always fight from a position of strength.

As you learn to love yourself, you become stronger, and the vampire will sense something different about you and react to it. I have seen cases where the wife became more powerful and confident to the point where the vampire backed off to avoid the stronger person she had become.

God will empower you. If you use that power, you overcome evil with good. You overcome the lie with the truth. Faith is the victory that overcomes the world. "I can do all things in Him [Christ] who strengthens me." (Philippians 4:13, RSV)

If you decide to leave, know that it is usually an ordeal. There may be everything from weeping, wailing, and gnashing of teeth to promises to change and offers to do whatever it takes. There may be threats and accusations and vicious, verbal assaults. Worse still, you may see all the above, which tend to cycle. Marriage vampires plead until they get mad, then attack until they revert to begging.

I encourage my clients to research the laws of their state, make their decisions, and fight to win. Your state may mandate legal issues regarding money, property, and children. In Texas, where I live, most parents share custody. Marriage vampires or not, most parents will have visitation rights if they don't have the primary residence for the children. Brace yourself. The marriage vampire will be involved in your kids' lives for years to come. Prepare for that reality.

In a community property state, both parents have rights regarding their children. Neither parent can simply decide with whom the children will live or where they attend school. If the parents cannot agree, visitation and parental rights will be determined in court, where the judge or jury will decide what is in the children's best interest.

If no legal guidelines exist, nasty legal court battles may occur—and the narcissist will do his best to charm counsel and the judge. You will hear lie after lie and will feel like you're being gaslit all over again. If he doesn't have an NPD diagnosis by a licensed professional or physician, you may not be able to use that information during the process.

I have often spoken with attorneys about the disorder to let them know what they're up against and decide how to proceed. Everything depends on your state's family code laws and your attorney's knowledge about the personality disorder and its potential danger to the family.

Vampires may fight their wives to the death in court while others just walk away. It is difficult to predict what will occur as each case is different.

I worked in a situation where the woman left, and the husband fought bitterly in court for custody of the children. They spent tens of thousands of dollars in legal fees in a court battle that dragged on until one day he just said, "Never mind," and walked away, telling his wife he didn't have any interest in the kids, and she could "keep" them.

I have also seen vampires who fought to "win" custody of the children to try to take them away from their mother if she chose to defy him. If a narcissist is determined and has money, this can be a challenging, emotionally draining experience. Even if you win, it may not be over. Some mothers "give up," and others will fight for years. I had mothers fight, only to have their children later jump ship to live with Dad, who promised them a "better deal."

No matter what happens, be true to yourself, do what is in the best interest of your children, and leave the rest in God's hands.

Stories from Women Who've Been There

The following three stories show what happens when wives of a marriage vampire set boundaries in relationships. I cannot emphasize this enough; my job is to empower the partner of a marriage vampire to become strong enough to set boundaries and enforce them. Only then will she see the redeeming possibilities God has for her life.

Story No. 1

I counseled a client married to a husband who had decided she needed to lose weight. She was not overweight for her age and was healthy. He just decided he wanted her back to her high school weight. This was not such an easy endeavor after having two children. Her husband began to monitor her weight morning, noon, and night. He would call her from work and ask what she had for lunch. He also was very particular about her hairstyle and the clothing she wore.

He called her one day to ask what she'd eaten for lunch. She told him she'd eaten a ham sandwich. Ham wasn't on the list of foods she could eat, he said, adding that he wanted her thinner and was embarrassed to be seen with her. His following words were a threat: "If you don't straighten up, I'll find someone else!"

"I wanted a ham sandwich," she replied coolly. "I am not going to diet anymore. I'm thin enough."

Her husband began swearing at her, telling her she was an unattractive, worthless piece of dirt. If she didn't get back on a diet, he said, he'd never have sex with her again. "That is ok if that's your decision," she replied. "I am a good wife and mother of two children, and everyone else tells me that I look good. You do not have to call me at lunch anymore. I'm going to hang up the phone now. Bye."

Her marriage vampire immediately got in his car and headed home to put her in her place. As he flung open the door, he began to rant and scream. His anger escalated, and he threatened to leave her, pull all her financial support, and take the kids. He had never assaulted her, but his face reddened as he went nose to nose with her, telling her she was worthless. He stormed out, slammed the door, and did not come home that night.

When the kids came home from school, she didn't tell them anything about the conflict. When they asked where their dad was, she replied unemotionally, "I don't know."

The following day, he called as if nothing had happened. "What do you weigh today?" he asked in a conversational tone. "Oh, I didn't weigh myself," she replied. "I'm not going to do that anymore, remember?"

He slammed down the phone, called the bank, and transferred all the money from their joint account into his new bank account.

She stood her ground. She knew the situation was escalating to the point of the ridiculous and, if it lasted very much longer, she would have to file for divorce just to get the judge to release funds so she and the kids could have enough money to survive.

By the end of the week, however, he returned. He walked in the door as if nothing had ever happened and her weight had never been an issue. He never brought it up again. He did, of course, become withdrawn and pouty. He also tried to control her through money and purposely did things to frustrate her. Then, one day, she caught him messing around with another woman, and that was that. She left him.

This was a situation where the woman was secure in herself. She was well armored. Even with all that, she couldn't hold the marriage together. To me, this woman was victorious. Success, or victory, is not necessarily keeping an abusive marriage together. Success is getting your life back, taking control of your esteem, making the right choices, and breathing again.

You cannot start at the bottom and go down. This woman did not have a good marriage. A woman should learn to love *herself*, not make a man love *her*.

She may not have her big, beautiful home or nice car anymore, but she has freedom, is no longer constantly criticized, berated, or attacked. She has peace of mind—something that no one can take from her unless she gives it away.

Story #2

She was a physical therapist, and he was an assistant pro-football coach. She was impressed with his position. They were both good-looking and were immediately attracted to each other. They married after a whirlwind courtship, and he whisked her away on a romantic Hawaiian honeymoon. When they returned home, all was well with the world. Months later, she became pregnant.

One day, she received an invitation to a special lunch with her husband and the football staff in the executive dining suite at the stadium. She entered the elevator with one other woman. After the door closed behind them, the woman quickly told her that she worked for the team as a temporary worker and disclosed she had also had an affair with the woman's husband. "I'd leave that no-good scum if I were you," the other woman said. The wife exclaimed, "But I'm pregnant!" The woman looked her in the eye and said, "In that case, never mind," and exited the elevator on the next floor.

The wife got off on the top floor, found her husband, and confronted him about this woman. His response was cool and calculated. "Oh, honey, that was just a crazy woman!" he said. "What would possess me to have a relationship with someone from work? That would be unprofessional. We are constantly on guard, especially with part-time people trying to stir up trouble and always needing a little more money." She believed him and went home, relieved.

Soon after, the baby came. His job required him to travel occasionally. One day, he came home from a trip and as she was unpacking his suitcase, she discovered condoms. As they'd never used condoms, she became distraught.

When she confronted him, this time, he went ballistic. "I cannot believe that you do not trust me!" he yelled. "Those are not mine. Someone from the hotel must have put them there. It must have been a sick joke the guys pulled on me. I'll find out who did this and put a stop to it."

She backed off.

Feeling that he might be right, she decided to contact my office for counseling. Still not sure what was happening, she told her story. She desperately wanted to trust her husband because the alternative was unthinkable.

When I advised her not to throw her brains on the floor and said, "I hate to tell you this, but it's obvious to everyone but you that this guy is a creep. Either you will have to deal with him now, or things will worsen. If you allow his sexual promiscuity, what kind of garbage do you think he will bring home next? It will not be easy to catch this guy, and you may be threatened with everything in the book. But if you stand your ground, things might change."

She did nothing. The situation escalated to a higher level of intensity when, one day, she accidentally picked up his phone, thinking it was hers. In her face was a text message from a woman: "Missin' u! Can't wait 'til next time!"

Again, the wife confronted her husband, and again, he became enraged, saying she had violated his privacy. He tried to persuade her that it was nothing and said if she didn't quit her paranoid behavior, he would leave her.

She decided she'd had enough and was prepared and ready for battle. "No, I'm the one who's going to leave you!" she announced.

That was all it took to crack his shell. As soon as she made that threat, he broke down and began to cry. "Please don't go!" he begged. "I'll never do this again!"

He appeared sincere. After a beautiful dinner out on the town, she reassured him she wouldn't leave if he would agree to go to counseling.

They did their best to work on the relationship in the following months and attended counseling together regularly. He told the counselor he was so happy that his wife was observant enough to catch this problem "in the nick of time."

He reassured them these were just mishaps, flirtations that had gotten out of hand.

However, one night, he left for work and inadvertently left his computer running. The wife went to his desk to check his computer to find out if he'd contacted other women. She saw an extensive history of porn sites as well as one that read, "Married and looking for partners."

Even after all his previous episodes of unfaithfulness, she expressed surprise at each new incident, as she genuinely believed his promises had been sincere. And wouldn't you know, all he had to say was, "No big deal, porn is porn. It's not like I am being unfaithful. That website is a joke. It's all make-believe fantasy stuff."

This time she wasn't going to let his actions slide. She obtained a copy of his computer's hard drive and made a list of all his "fantasy" leads. She contacted other women who confessed they had engaged in casual sex with her husband. Now she was armed with the truth. "Poor me" was not going to work anymore.

When she met him head-on, he began to lash out at her. He told her he had started to stray because she was not meeting his needs in bed anymore and that *she* was the cause of all of this. He told her if she didn't change, he'd hit the road. This made her nervous because she knew his threats were plausible—and he had all the income. She'd never be able to afford the lifestyle to which she had become accustomed on her own.

It was time to put on her armor. She decided she would no longer play his game. She was prepared when he threatened to move out, file for divorce, and take their child. She hired an attorney, gave his office a copy of her husband's computer hard drive, filed for divorce, and informed her husband that her attorney would subpoena the women he'd been involved with and bring them to court to testify under oath.

He had a nervous breakdown, became suicidal, and was treated in a psychiatric ward.

When a narcissist's ego defenses are pierced, such as when they become trapped in their lies, caught with evidence, or caught in the act, they may fall apart, become depressed, appear psychotic, or become suicidal. I refer to that as "breaking the oyster shell." It shows that the formidable ego defenses or walls they have constructed throughout their lifetime are broken or temporarily breached.

When a marriage vampire's shell cracks and his lies no longer work, those walls cannot protect him anymore. The world was about to see who this man indeed was, and the revelation was explosive. He was desperate, and instead of exposure in court, he confessed everything to her and begged her to please take him back. "If you divorce me, everyone will know what an idiot I am!"

He came clean on all the infidelity, even confessing he had solicited prostitutes on his travels. He admitted to having sex with women he met online. She was appalled and unsure what to do next.

Her husband was remorseful and wanted to die. But the woman was strong, and at least she now knew the whole truth. She took him back only after he agreed to marriage counseling, as well as treatment for his sexual addiction.

Things were OK ... for a while. "I'm well now," he claimed. "The therapy was great, and now I can manage on my own."

Slowly, his ego defenses began to return, and he started to reinterpret his past deeds: He'd had sex with women, but not many. He began to blame his past for his behavior. She correctly interpreted his arrogance as a red flag and demanded the right to monitor him again. Feeling invincible, he shot back, "Aren't you a Christian? I thought you had forgiven me for all that stuff. None of that counts anymore. Aren't you supposed to trust me?"

Again, he threatened to divorce her. She stood her ground. She now knew his ploys and remained firm. Instead of submitting to his threats, she filed for divorce.

"Don't do this to me!" he begged, on the verge of another breakdown. He was readmitted to an in-patient treatment facility.

She forced him into treatment, and this time they began to deal with his narcissistic traits. This included giving her access to all his communications—phone, emails, and the computer.

They are still hanging together. He did not stray again, as far as I know, but she was on high alert constantly in case he did stray. She confessed that their relationship is less like a marriage and more like a mother constantly monitoring a rebellious, impulsive teenager.

She knew who she was in the Lord, and she held her ground. By forcing her husband to become transparent, she stopped his cheating but remained vigilant, which can be an exhausting way to live. That was her choice and how she decided to live.

Story #3

This stay-at-home mom had a domineering husband. He constantly belittled her worth by telling her she was a bad mother, a lousy cook, and an inept time manager. He didn't care who was in the room to hear his exhaustive diatribes.

At her insistence, they met with me in my offices. The husband berated his wife in a session for not telling him how long the session would take. "You never do anything right!" He attacked her verbally in front of me, their therapist.

This woman had had enough! She realized her husband was using the session as an attempt to control and embarrass her, hoping his behavior would prevent her from seeking counseling. She decided to seek individual therapy to change herself and her situation.

Again, if someone has freedom of choice, you cannot force changed behaviors. Here is what she did: She realized the truth about herself, became stronger—physically, mentally, and spiritually—and decided to stand up to him. She also realized she was getting nowhere fast, and her kids and immediate family had lost respect for her. She became the brunt of all his jokes. It was like living with a high school bully.

After counseling, she could unemotionally tell her husband that she would leave him if he didn't stop criticizing her. She stood her ground. Remember ... I said that things might escalate when you stand up for yourself. He became angry and moved out of their bedroom, but not the house. He schemed to turn the children against her by playing the generous dad.

Despite his manipulation, she held her ground and continued to be the mom she'd always been. She made breakfast, took the kids to school, and did her daily chores.

One day, she received divorce papers. He demanded full custody of the kids in the documents and tried to paint her as a terrible mother. He wanted the house and the kids so that she'd have to pay child support. She had been a mother of two (ages fourteen and sixteen) for sixteen years and never had an outside job. In Texas, a twelve-year-old can petition the judge, a fourteen-year-old can have an audience with the judge, and a sixteen-year-old can petition a judge to live with the parent they prefer. A judge is responsible for deciding what is in the child's best interests, not delivering what a child (or the narcissist) wants.

With the "counsel" of a brilliant friend, the husband had a plan. He had secretly been "working" on the children, trying to persuade them to live with him. The husband promised his sixteen-year-old son that he would buy him a new car if he came to live with him. He convinced the boy to tell the judge he wanted to live with the father. The man planned to appeal to the courts that the children needed to remain together, not be separated.

The wife hired an attorney even though she did not have the money. The situation looked grim until the fourteen-year-old daughter refused to play ball with dad. The judge determined there would be joint custody, the house would go on sale with proceeds split, and the husband would pay all the legal fees.

Dad quickly remarried, and his new wife despised the son. He tried to keep the boy with him, but the friction between the son and new wife was too great. The son moved back in with his mom, and the tables changed again.

The ex-husband now had to pay total child support and alimony. He cut off college support for the children, just as he had cut them off emotionally when they had not co-operated with the plan.

You cannot keep a good warrior down. Mom held on, never flinched, and never gave up. She received incredible support from her family and a prayer group at church. She did not get the house or the car, but she is free. She realized she was intelligent, not the idiot her husband unceasingly accused her of being.

She says she feels reborn, like a breath of fresh air! She goes to the store, buys groceries, and is not criticized for every single move she makes. "So if the Son [Christ] sets you free, you will be free indeed." (John 8:36, NIV)

This was not the marriage she signed up for because there was no love. She had expected treatment as any human should. She erected barriers to protect herself when she realized her husband could not love her. She stood her ground, and he had to leave. Was she afraid for the future? Yes, at first. But when she could breathe again, she knew she could do it. She wrapped her armor around herself and stepped into a future filled with hope.

What Defines You

Who will set the boundaries for your life? Your partner? Your spouse? The culture? Who determines how close I stand to you? Who tells you what you should do? Who gets to put their hands on you? Who decides what you read, what you watch, what you believe?

Boundaries do not just protect you; they define you. Declare your boundaries and prepare for the fight to come. You will be fighting for yourself. You will be protecting yourself. No one can tell you where to set the boundaries, and you can change them.

You can love and respect yourself. Either you decide how long you will debate an issue, or the marriage vampire will. You decide what you will do, say, and think about yourself, or the marriage vampire will. You decide who will set your boundaries—if not, you will wish you had.

The United States has maritime limits and boundaries beyond its borders by the Laws of the Sea. The territorial sea extends twelve nautical miles from the low-water line of our coasts. If you were an adversary and crossed that line with your ship, you'd be in our territorial waters. We could board your boat and arrest you if you broke our laws. If you were on a warship, we could sink you as we did in World War II. To declare a boundary is one thing, but you must also be willing to challenge or confront those who cross that boundary. *You must defend your boundary.*

Battle Prayer for Victory

Dear Lord,
I thank You for Your Word.
I thank You for the love You have declared for me.
You bought me for a price, and that price was the blood of Your only Son.
You have called me to stand; stand with me.
You have promised me Your armor; protect me.
You have given me Your Word; instruct me.
You have promised me Your strength; sustain me.
You have given me Your Spirit; fill me.
Open my heart to know Your love.
Open my eyes to see that You have given me the victory.
Then, no matter how desperate the battle, there is never a sign that You do not love me.
These are the lies of the evil one. His flaming darts will not wound me, for You are with me always.
Peace comes from You and cannot be taken away.
I will stand today. Stand with me.
The victory is mine. It cannot be taken away.
I will not give it away.
In Your Son's Name, Amen.

8

The Battle Is Joined

"In all things we are more than conquerors
through Him who loved us."
(Romans 8:37, RSV)

Now that you have decided to engage the vampire, you must choose when and where to fight. You have put on your armor and must be ready to go into battle with measured expectations. We know the effect the conflict will have on the vampire. What impact will the battle have on *you*?

People may prepare for battle using anger. Others feel fear. Both emotions release adrenaline, which makes you feel more powerful. Anger may feel good, but it distracts your mind. Anger reduces your strength and undermines your health. Fear or anger are heavy. They are extra burdens in life's battles. Why add to the marriage vampire's wounds with self-induced ones?

Some may say, "Get angry, girl! Get angry!" This just makes things worse. The Bible calls these emotions "strongholds." They get you riled up inside but should not be used before, during, or after the battle.

Anger is not in God's arsenal. Anger and fear are the ammunition of the enemy. Satan has used these tools for millennia to help people destroy others in fits of rage. If we use anger and fear for motivation, we will leave our shoes of peace behind. It is Satan's hope and desire that you cling to these emotions. When you do, he wins. You have chosen to walk in his destructive ways and not on the path of God's promises, provision, and plans for you.

"Be angry but do not sin; do not let the sun go down on your anger, and give no opportunity to the devil." (Ephesians 4:26-27, RSV)

Letting go of anger during battle is the essential thing the partner of a vampire can do.

Why Does Anger Feel Good?

Anger is an adrenaline response to a wound—physical or mental. Initially, it makes you feel strong and creates a fight response. It affects every part of your body: Your heart beats faster, your lungs breathe deeper, your eyes dilate to a wider field of vision, your muscles tense, and you have increased energy. Acid pours into your stomach to quickly generate additional fuel. Blood moves from your hands and feet and is redirected to your heart, lungs, and brain to help you deal with the threat. All this would come in handy if attacked by a mountain lion. The sad thing is that your body cannot distinguish between a mountain lion and a screaming husband.

Anger becomes heavier and heavier as more offenses are added to the list by the marriage vampire. The anger you carry does nothing to change the offender. If you maintain this level of anger as a defensive shield, it creates more stress, and your body begins to wear out.

Stress is like putting air in a balloon. Inflating a balloon applies pressure to the whole system, but the balloon pops at the point where the material is weakest. The same thing happens to the human body. Stress shows up where we are physically most vulnerable. It may be ulcers; others develop high blood pressure, heart problems, headaches, or irritable bowel syndrome. When we attempt to defend ourselves through anger, we destroy our bodies.

Anything you can do with anger, you can do without anger. Anything you can do with fear, you can do without fear. You can fight. You can flee. You can stand your ground. You can give in if it does not damage you. You can do whatever is wise to do. Do what is most effective, and do not let emotions distract you.

"Let us also lay aside every weight, and sin which clings so closely, and let us run with perseverance the race that is set before us..." (Hebrews 12:1, RSV)

God does not get heart attacks or ulcers. God the Father is a spiritual being not limited by the physical body. God can carry the weight of the world. Humans are not created to carry that burden. God also firmly declares—not suggests—"Vengeance is mine, I will repay, says the Lord." (Romans 12:19, RSV)

Vengeance is not in your job description. Aren't you glad? If you want to live a long and happier life, let go of your anger and accept His offer of rest.

How Do I Let Go of Anger?

Letting go of anger isn't easy, especially if you've been seething in it for a long time, but you can do it!

How is this possible? Forgiveness! The only way to get rid of anger is through forgiveness.

The biblical meaning of forgiveness is to "choose not to punish." Yes, you hurt. Yes, these events did happen to you. Do not search for ways to excuse the behaviors. You must simply decide not to punish, and the only way to do this is to let go of the offense.

The human brain retains everything. That is the way God created it. You cannot just "forgive and forget." Otherwise, you must deny your brain's purpose is to remember things. To believe something didn't happen when it did is psychotic. We cannot make it go away. What you can do, however, is to decide that each time you recall the offense, you can also remember your decision not to punish.

If we try to protect ourselves with anger, we are reliving the events, continually reminding ourselves that we were victims, making us unable to move forward.

"Repay no one evil for evil, but take thought for what is noble in the sight of all. If possible, so far as it depends upon you, live peaceably with all. Beloved, never avenge yourselves, but leave it to the wrath of God; for it is written, 'Vengeance is mine, I will repay, says the Lord.' No, 'if your enemy is hungry, feed him; if he is thirsty, give him drink; for by so doing you will heap burning coals upon his head.' Do not be overcome by evil, but overcome evil with good." (Romans 12:17-21, RSV)

Our mission is to overcome evil with good. Not to get even. Not to harm. Not to beat our adversary into submission. Not to feel more powerful.

It makes us think: What is anger suitable for? Absolutely nothing. Walk away from anger no matter where it comes from.

In fact, instead of storing ammunition for the next assault, look for opportunities to bless your adversary. Do not give in to his lies but bless him. Why?

"...for you will heap coals of fire on his head, and the Lord will reward you." (Proverbs 25:22, RSV)

Letting Go of Fear

Fear is another unhealthy emotion that generates adrenalin. Never take flight because of fear. Take flight because it is the wise thing to do. Fear is the sister to anxiety. More women tend to struggle with fear than with anger. You may worry about what will happen if you stand up to your marriage vampire. Worrying about what could happen will get you nowhere. The only thing worrying changes is you. And the response to worry will weaken you.

If you're afraid the roof will leak, fear doesn't make a hole in the roof. It also doesn't fix a hole in the roof if one exists. What does your fear or apprehension do to the roof? Absolutely nothing. If there is something you can do to improve your life, do it. If there is nothing you can do, give it to God. Pray, and He will hear you. Give Him your anxieties.

God's truth shines the light on the dark things you are afraid of, like turning on a light to assure a child no monsters are lurking under the bed. God tells you that He is in charge, and you do not have to be afraid anymore. Stop wondering if you are going to make it.

You can live and be free from worry.

The scripture below is the key to combating fear. These words come right out of Jesus's mouth. He spoke to people living under a cruel and unjust dictator. Not only were the people experiencing financial struggles, but they felt spiritual concerns that God did not love them because of their poverty. The religious elite of the day had convinced the people that material wealth was a sign of God's favor. Only by following the elites' spiritual dictates could anyone access God's blessing. The people were at the mercy of these blind guides. Where could they turn, and what could they do to escape this impossible burden? Jesus provides the answer:

"Therefore I tell you, do not worry about your life, what you will eat or what you will drink, or about your body, what you will wear. Is not life more than food, and the body more than clothing? Look at the birds of the air; they neither sow nor reap nor gather into barns, and yet your heavenly Father feeds them. Are you not of more value than they? And can any of you by worrying add a single hour to your span of life? And why do you worry about clothing? Consider the lilies of the field, how they grow; they neither toil nor spin, yet I tell you, even Solomon in all his glory was not clothed like one of these. But if God so clothes the grass of the field, which is alive today and tomorrow is thrown into the oven, will he not much more clothe you—you of little faith? Therefore do not worry, saying, 'What will we eat?' or 'What will we drink?' or 'What will we wear?' For it is the Gentiles who strive for all these things; and indeed your heavenly Father knows that you need all these things. But strive first for the kingdom of God and His righteousness, and all these things will be given to you as well. So do not worry about tomorrow, for tomorrow will bring worries of its own. Today's trouble is enough for today." (Matthew 6:25-34, NRSV)

In Matthew 14, during a storm, the apostles became afraid. Jesus told them, "Take heart, it is I; have no fear." Christ invited Peter to walk on water to Him, and Peter did that... until he became afraid. Then Peter began to sink and cried out to Christ to save him. Christ reached out His hand and rescued Peter, asking '...o man of little faith, why did you doubt?'" (Matthew 14:27-31, RSV).

Exercising your faith dispels fear. Peter was initially afraid to get out of his boat in the storm. I would have been, too. He called out to Jesus and got the OK to step out onto the water. Peter moved his feet, one foot in front of the other, to walk toward Christ. Now that is faith! He believed what Jesus told him and then acted on it. He walked on water. This is exercising your faith. God gives you His armor, His plan, His open door, and His okay. Then suddenly, you may become fearful. That is the time to exercise your faith.

As long as Peter's focus remained on Christ and Peter believed he could do it, he could. It was when Peter lost that faith that he began to sink.

When you feel fearful, that's your signal to begin to exercise your faith and knowledge of the truth. God's Word is His proof of faithfulness. God tells us that fear lacks faith in His promise to sustain and give us victory. Faith is the victory that overcomes the world.

In Hebrews 3, God told His people they could not enter into the land God had promised them because of their unbelief. They had sent twelve spies to scout the land of Canaan. Ten spies told the people they were not strong enough to defeat the Canaanites. Because they didn't believe in themselves or God's promises, the people wandered in the wilderness for forty years. They saw themselves as weak and thought they could not win. They chose fear over God's promises and stayed in the wilderness for the rest of their lives. Their children conquered the land and became the recipients of God's blessings.

When God says you can win, believe God! Believe God even if the marriage vampire tells you that you can't win.

When God says you can win, believe God! Even if you begin to fear and tell yourself you can't win, believe God instead.

That's what this book is about... believing what God tells you, not what the narcissist says or your own doubts. Believe God instead.

It is so important to "Trust in the Lord with all your heart, and do not rely on your own insight. In all your ways acknowledge him, and he will make straight your paths." (Proverbs 3:5-6, RSV)

Truth Is Your Greatest Weapon!

When the battle presents itself, and you're ready to stand your ground, bravely tell the truth. Tell your vampire the boundary lines, what you are willing to do and what you are no longer going to do.

Do not start if you cannot finish. If you say you will not pick up the newspaper, do not walk out the door to retrieve it. If you tell him you're not going to allow him to abuse or degrade you by forcing you to participate in uncomfortable sexual practices, then stand your ground and don't let him convince you to do anything that makes you feel uncomfortable. He designed his insults to distract, wound, and punish you. He wants to hurt you so that you will submit to him.

Defending yourself is not as effective as staying on the issue—and the answer is "No." Do not allow yourself to be baited into debating his charges, allegations, and lies. Ignore them all, dig in, and stay on the issue.

No more debating for hours. No more losing sleep. Say "No." Say it repeatedly if needed. Hold on until it is over. That's why you should choose the time and the place for the battle if possible.

If you choose to battle in public, the initial effect might be different, as he likely will not act so angrily in public. Understand, however, there is a price you will pay when you get home. Be prepared to pay it. You will begin to see that it is the same old song and dance—repeatedly. If you don't give in and fight back, he will exhaust himself... eventually.

9

Forgiving Is For-Giving

"Do not be overcome with evil,
but overcome evil with good."
(Romans 12:21, RSV)

We consciously choose to forgive when we decide not to punish others. We can let go of offenses fully and completely. You do not forgive people because they deserve it; you forgive them because *you* deserve to move on with your life! That may be difficult, but it's smart.

One Child's Story

He was the fifth of seven children. His father was an alcoholic and was a narcissist. His mother was a committed Christian who took her seven children to church every time the doors were open. They walked both ways because they did not have a car. They were poor.

The boy's mother never used foul language, lied, or acted in any violent manner. She tried to be a good Christian. The boy's father frequently yelled, cussed, lied, or drank himself into a stupor. As a dock worker, the boy's father was increasingly unable to obtain work at the docks because of his "impairments." His lack of work options meant he would lie around the house more often, drink more, and become increasingly physically abusive to his wife and children.

With five children in five years, and her husband working less and less, you can imagine the economic hardship the boy's family experienced. His mother knew how to stick up for herself, though, and she protected her children. "Shut up, Red, you're drunk," she would tell his father when he would start in on one of his tirades. She did not hesitate to call the police if he tried to hit her.

Despite the father's behavior, he was the boy's hero. He told stories about everything, but the boy especially loved his dad's war stories because his dad claimed to have fought in every battle and on every front. He seemed to know everything—about stars and lizards and the best fishing holes in Texas. You can imagine the boy's mixed feelings when his dad, who treated this boy as his "favorite," would go crazy and lash out at someone or break something. These episodes came out of nowhere. It was like flipping a switch. His dad would go from easygoing to "wild man" at the slightest provocation.

Strangely enough, the boy did not receive the abuse his older brother and sisters received. His dad was a man without rules, and like many narcissists, his father enjoyed fighting. When he was seven, the boy witnessed his dad beating his older brother with a broomstick.

That traumatic episode changed the boy's life. At that moment, he decided he would never become the target of his father's rage. If the father said, "Stop!" the boy stopped. If he said, "Frog," the boy jumped. If his dad started talking through clenched teeth, it meant things would get worse, and it was time for the boy to get as far away as possible.

His father's behavior worsened. The boy noticed that his dad's war stories were the same themes they watched in "B" movies on TV. The boy was also surprised to learn that his father had not been injured seven times in World War

II. He hadn't been shot at all! His father had received a Purple Heart, not for a dangerous battle fight, but after being knocked off his Army tank and dislocating his shoulder during wartime.

When the boy was ten years old, his mom had her seventh and last child. There had now been several "episodes" in which his mother had fled the home and enlisted the help of relatives to hide her children. She was forced to flee for her life alone on multiple occasions. After one particularly intense fight with his father, the police were called, and she left with all her children. She walked down the road with seven children ranging in age from an infant to the oldest son, who was fifteen years old. This time she didn't come back. She knew she must protect her children from their father. She divorced him.

The boy's father had grown increasingly mean, angry, and violent. It was a relief for the boy to be away from him. He sang a song about being "thankful to God and Greyhound" [bus] that his father was finally out of the picture and no longer posed an immediate threat to his mother or the family. (It was a rendition of country singer Roy Clark's song, "Thank God and Greyhound You're Gone," 1970).

His family lived with an aunt and uncle for about a year, and his mom went to work at a manufacturing plant. His father contributed nothing to their support, and soon his mother began to be afraid she would lose her kids. Even with the financial stresses, her biggest fear was her children's education. She believed that education was the only way out of poverty.

Although the boy's father was a poor excuse for a man, his mother taught her four sons the truth. She was not critical of her husband, but she told them what good men do—and don't do. "Good men don't drink," she told them. "Good men do not beat their wives. Good men provide for their families."

The boy moved to a Christian children's home when he was eleven. One sibling was already living at the children's home, and the mother and remaining siblings moved there months later. His mother became an employee of the children's home. He never saw his father again. His dad died when the boy was eighteen. Now the threat of having his father show up unexpectedly to talk his way back into their lives was gone. If you had asked the boy at that time, he would have said he was angry with his father and was glad he was dead. He said this in defense of his mother, whom the father had beaten and driven into poverty.

Eight years later, the boy had a conversation with his mother and was stunned to find that she was not angry at his father one bit. She told him his father was the only man she had ever loved and that the only reason she had left him was to protect the kids. She was not worried about herself. She stood toe-to-toe with him and never backed down. "He was such a liar!" the son insisted. To his surprise, she chuckled. "Oh, that was just Red. If I ever found out that something he said was true, I was amazed."

The young man left that conversation quite distressed. It was foolish for him to hold onto a grudge on behalf of his mother, who was not disturbed or angry. He began to explore why he was so angry with his father. After introspection, he realized he was angry because he loved his father very much but felt that his father never loved him. When the young man finally let go of that anger, he learned he could stop holding people at arm's length and soon began to open up to others. He decided he would choose a life path different from his father's, and he would never treat his wife or children the way his father had treated him or his mother, brothers, or sisters.

I was the boy in this story. Years later, I realized that some people have no love in them, and it is impossible to give what one does not have. It still hurts, but it is good to know it was not something I did. My father was just "made that way." And because I was the boy in this story, I can and do understand what you are going through. It is why I have spent my entire life trying to help people make sense of their lives. I want others to understand what it is like for children of a parent who has NPD.

If You Decide to Stay

If you decide to stay, then what? Can you protect yourself and your children? Is it worth the fight? There isn't any rule that says wives of vampires must leave, divorce their spouses, or do anything else, for that matter. Marriage vampires make rotten partners and tend to be difficult to change. You have a choice: You can go and fight, or you can stay and fight.

I tell my clients that I will help them protect themselves if they decide to leave or stay in the marriage—whichever they choose. I do not make that decision for them.

Clients come to me after vampire spouses have threatened them with divorce or after they have already separated. I tell them, "I'll help you get him back. But if you do get him back, you probably will not have the man you want. You'll get the vampire who left."

You may question this, but the fact is, a woman may love her vampire husband. There is nothing wrong with that. Most vampires work hard to look like the people they're expected to be, and as there is no problem with the ability of these women to love, they may decide to stay and take their chances that their partner will change.

When you make your decision, you may receive criticism from unexpected sources. Friends or family may urge you to leave or remark that you do not respect yourself if you choose to remain in a dead-end relationship.

I'm not willing to suggest such a thing, but I do hope the reason you have chosen to stay is due to LOVE. If you remain for any other reason, you need to get help. Do not stay out of fear. Do not stay out of obligation. Do not stay out of desperation, and do not stay out of guilt.

A woman should never be forced to remain in a dangerous marriage. That is simply not in the Bible and is of no value to you as a Christian spouse. God says so. It is right there in I Corinthians 13. If you do things out of any other motive than love, it is of no value to you. Do not choose to be a martyr; you will only wear yourself out.

If you stay because you are afraid of what the vampire might do, figure out a way to defend yourself and then leave. If you are staying out of guilt, forgive yourself and move on with your life. If you believe this is the best you can expect because "you are such a worthless person," stop listening to the lies of the vampire and Satan. Listen to God, who wants you to believe in what He thinks of you. However, if you choose to stay, please do so because you have found a way to love yourself and that you are aware of, accept, and understand the cost and challenges ahead of you.

You Need to Prepare

As a child in the small Texas town of Medina, doing farm work in my overalls and brogans, a former supervisor used to say to me, "Tomorrow you'd better wear tennis shoes and bring a light lunch because we're going to be hauling hay."

The wives of vampires will need armor and a source of spiritual renewal each day if they intend to stay and fight the symptoms of narcissism day in and day out. It is going to be work, challenging work! Put on your tennis shoes and bring a light lunch! Doing things out of love will allow you to hang in there, but what will be your source of love? The fact is that the only source of love is God and those who come to know Him.

NPDs lack empathy and are unable to give love. It is just not in them. But you can love your vampire if you maintain your source of power and are ready to start the battle each new day, protected and powerful.

"But if the Spirit of Him who raised Jesus from the dead dwells in you, He who raised Christ from the dead will also give life to your mortal bodies through His Spirit who dwells in you." (Romans 8:11, NKJV)

God made His Spirit live within you, and that Spirit will make you alive! He will give you the power to do what is right and good and will renew your strength each day.

"The Lord is my portion," says my soul, "therefore I will hope in him." (Lamentations 3:24, RSV). The Spirit is there to help us. God also says, "fear not, for I am with you, be not dismayed, for I am your God; I will strengthen you, I will help you, I will uphold you with my victorious right hand." (Isaiah 41:10, RSV)

The word portion means "share." We get our share from God, and our hope comes from Him, not from ourselves or the marriage vampire. The great news is that this "share" is *new each morning*! You can wake up refreshed, revived, and ready to deal with all the lies Satan throws at you.

On the other hand, I have had clients who chose to stay with their husbands and later decided it wasn't worth a lifetime of enduring daily conflict and unpredictable behavior.

Most women do not marry to spend their lives protecting themselves or bracing themselves for the next lie, manipulation, or betrayal that comes along. They want to be happy. They want to love and be loved. They do not want to exhaust themselves from caring for fragile little boys who constantly lie. They do not want to be considered a token wife or a controlling mother.

Other women told me that once they put on their armor, found support, and stood up for themselves, they were able to deal with the NPD effectively, even though it was like having another child to raise.

Pray Out Loud

Vampires come in all stripes; some are less aggressive than others. Some become suffering martyrs, and it's like pushing a rope to get them to do anything. Some are forced to change or leave. The results are mixed, but all the studies indicate that NPDs don't tend to change, and if they do, they don't change much. The bulk of the change in the relationship will be coming from you.

You will have to start each day renewing your spirit with God's truth. You may want to begin with a devotional. Store up in your memory all the beautiful things that God says about you.

It helps to have a support system, a mentor, or a group that encourages and reminds you of who you are in God's eyes. You will need to pray—out loud—and claim the love He gives you, the armor He has provided, and the weapons "not of this world" to capture every negative thought.

You can think the truth about yourself each time the vampire bites you. What if every time a marriage vampire criticized his wife, she was able to recite these verses mentally?

"Bless those who persecute you; bless and do not curse them...Do not be overcome by evil, but overcome evil with good." (Romans 12:14-21, RSV)

If your mind automatically recalls the truth, you can respond more effectively and lovingly.

Don't Get Even

If you find yourself becoming angry, resentful, or tired, it may not be because of your wounds. It may be that you are frustrated—a different source of anger—because you find yourself going through the same old thing repeatedly.

Remember, staying was your choice. You made a conscious decision to remain and do the best you can. The option should always be yours—not his, not your family's, and not the well-meaning people who believe you ought to leave.

Do what is right for *you*. Later, if you decide your decision is no longer the best, you always have the freedom to change it again.

The longer you live with a marriage vampire, the more you want to get even. Do not fall into that trap. The goal is not merely to survive; it is to have life and have it more abundantly. You do not have to get even; you want to move forward in life!

Don't allow your life to be burdened by the wounds of a narcissist. Let go of this pain and move on. Anger and resentment feel like power because of the adrenaline rush they give your body, but they are burdens and are harmful to you, both emotionally and physically.

God instructs us to forgive, not because the narcissist deserves it, but because it benefits *you*. You can be free of the past by living in the "here and now" and looking forward to the future.

"Brethren, I do not consider that I have made it my own, but one thing I do, forgetting what lies behind and straining forward to what lies ahead, I press on toward the goal for the prize of the upward call of God in Christ Jesus." (Philippians 3:13-14, RSV)

You cannot out-criticize a vampire. You cannot out-lie, out-manipulate, or out-pout one—and you don't want to waste your time trying. You can only overcome evil with good. If you aren't going to avenge yourself, why keep a list? Why hold those things in your heart? Why drag them around like a sack of rocks? Why let them slow you down? It will only make your life heavy and sad.

Let me remind you of what Paul meant when he said, "Be angry but do not sin; do not let the sun go down on your anger, and give no opportunity to the devil." (Ephesians 4:26-27, RSV)

So, what do you do with it? You forgive it. This may seem crazy, but it is what we are instructed to do. Do not keep score. Forgive.

Forgiving is not what people think. I am not saying that a verbal jab doesn't hurt. I'm not saying his offenses are okay. But it is letting go of those offenses that allow us to survive another day. You will tend to collect these "wounds" rather than pull them out to stay well.

Remember, if you choose to remain to get even with him or beat him at his own game, you will do more damage to yourself. You will not survive if you leave his arrows in your heart. They will fester and infect your life, and you will be tempted to shoot those arrows back at him one day. You must pull those arrows out and let your heart heal.

If you are waiting until the enemy is down so you can get even, it's not worth your time. Quit dreaming about the day when you settle the score. You'll lose if you do. It is not a game you were meant to play.

I have heard the term "Let it go," as if the wounds were balloons that would fly away if you just let go of the string. Instead, we must pry and scrape the wounds off as if welded on. But you can do it. God showed us how. You choose not to punish.

The next time you see the person who hurt you, do not drag up your list so you can add today's insults to the ones you recorded yesterday. You choose not to get back at him for what he did. This does not mean you have to let that person keep hurting you. You do not have to trust him. That would be silly; he is not trustworthy. You do have to give up your dream of retaliating in any way. This will be hard because the human brain protects by recalling things that hurt. That is why we blow on hot chocolate before taking a sip; we remember scalding our tongue.

When you see people who hurt you, you recall the things they did. That is an instinctive defense to help you prevent experiencing the pain in the future. If feelings of anger or a desire for revenge come with those memories, you must remind yourself that you have chosen to forgive that offense. This is a command of God, not a suggestion. You will be "overcome by evil" if you do not learn to forgive. Each time you recall a wound, remember the cure: "I forgave that!" It works. It will take time, but then you will be ready for the next step—forbearing.

Forbearing

In Colossians 3:5-17, Paul lists a whole roster of emotional responses that we are to put to death, including "wrath, malice, and anger," as well as another series of traits we need to put on when dealing with a marriage vampire. Forbearance is listed along with love, compassion, and kindness. Forbearing means "controlling oneself when provoked." It means you don't take note of slights, attacks, and attempts to hurt. You just let those fiery darts bounce off your shield of faith, believing in God and having confidence in the knowledge of who you are.

You know the drill of a marriage vampire. If you cook, he will say the chicken is too dry. If you go out to eat, he wonders why you never have a home-cooked meal. Do you expect to find that your vampire is a "new" man, one who isn't arrogant, selfish, and demanding? If you are surprised every day, you haven't been paying attention. You don't have to keep a record of all the mean things he has said and done in retaliation. You can forbear.

Forbearance is like having a store's cashier say there is no charge for an item you have brought through the checkout line. It is not on your bill or charged to your account. It's free. When you become adept at forgiving, you give your vampire a free pass, and you don't count the offenses when he starts in on you. That's the reason this book was written—so you could forbear and get on with your life.

If you've ever asked someone to forgive you for a mistake or remark you made, and the person said, "Oh, I wasn't offended. Don't worry about that," weren't you relieved? You may have been dreading having to apologize. But now you think, "Whew! I am glad that is behind us!"

That is what Jesus does for you. He forgave your sins when you became a Christian. He now forbears your sin. He does not "charge" you for it. You are forgiven, your sins are not recorded, and you do not ever have to fear God in that way again.

Forgiveness and forbearance free us. We do not keep score; we do not want to get even; we do not devise evil plans in retaliation. We get to live in the here and now, and we get to do whatever is effective or noble in the sight of God and others.

I can tell you from my own experience that when I let go of the anger I had toward my dead father, I was able to let others get close to me. I could love and not waste my time or life trying to get revenge. I no longer felt the need to stay angry.

Let us let God heal us. Let us give ourselves a break and forgive as we have been forgiven. Let us forbear, patiently enduring whatever comes.

10

The New You

"She who was not loved, I will call my beloved."
(Romans 9:25, RSV)

I don't know what you know about boxing, but if the world's heavyweight champion announces that he'll defend his title against a contender, I can guarantee he will not be fighting that fight the very next week.

He'll schedule it for six months from now. Why so long? He wants time to prepare and be as strong as possible. He wants to be like Rocky. He will get in shape, practice with sparring partners, eat right, and sleep right. When he's ready, *then* he will fight. He dedicates his mind, energy, and time to the upcoming battle. He knows the preparation will help determine his success.

That is what I want you to do. To sustain a long emotional battle, you need a strong physical body. It is your platform for the fight, your foundation. You will need to take care of yourself. You are in the middle of one of the most challenging scenarios you will ever face. But you can do it! You have proven that you are capable and ready to tackle the most demanding stuff life can hand you. I hope you also know by now that I am on your side. But no one can stand with you if you cannot stand up!

Quit beating yourself up and start building yourself up to become strong and healthy. If someone says, "I hate you! You are worthless. You never do anything right!" we would consider that person to be mean, hostile, and angry.

But if someone says, "I hate my life! I am worthless. I never do anything right. I wish I could die ... in fact, I'm thinking of ways to kill myself!" we understand that person is depressed.

Hostility is anger turned outward. Depression is anger turned inward. Frequently, the partners of marriage vampires are depressed. Not sad. Depressed.

Fighting Depression

I teach clients that depression is not a mood; it is a biological illness. Depression is not feeling down or blue; it is a physical illness with observable symptoms. If you are sad, cheer up! If you are depressed, you have low serotonin levels in your brain, and you will have to increase your serotonin levels. Serotonin is a neurotransmitter in your brain, and oddly, in your digestive system. It helps your nerves function properly.

When your serotonin level is low, you begin to have problems with many things that make your life miserable. The wacky thing about depression is that the symptoms vary from person to person. They can be the opposite of the things you identify with depression. You may sleep too much or too little. You may lose your appetite or be ravenously hungry. You may overthink (racing thoughts) or feel like your mind is slogging through thick mud. You may feel lethargic, like you are swimming in lead, or feel like you are about to jump out of your skin. In either extreme, the symptoms represent a departure from normal functioning.

Most people with depression are despondent, with depressed moods and crying spells, self-doubt, guilt, low self-esteem, and may have suicidal ideation.

Others have a condition we call anhedonia. Anhedonia means "no pleasure in life." If you have this condition, nothing feels good. Nothing is worth the effort. You lose interest in everything you used to enjoy—reading, painting, tennis, going to the movies, or other activities. Your life may become blah, and there is nothing to which you look forward.

Depression in adults (and frequently in teens and children) is accompanied by being in an irritable mood. Everything bugs you, even things you used to ignore or not notice. You may see everyone as annoying. Depression shows up in various forms—from one emotional extreme to another.

Depressed people are hapless and hopeless.

Hapless means: "Good things never happen to me."

Hopeless means: "Good things are not going to start."

As you can imagine, that is not the attitude we want in a fighter.

A fighter needs to think she can win; she needs to believe she can make it and think she will reach her goal if she tries hard enough. That is what I want for you. Even if you do not always win, you will come closer to obtaining what you want. It is hard to motivate people who believe they cannot win.

If you are depressed, you'll need to increase your serotonin levels to get up to fighting speed.

Exercise is Nature's Antidepressant

When you are in balance, your brain produces serotonin. Balanced sleep, diet, and exercise lead to higher serotonin levels. When you do not keep these three in balance, you experience a downward cycle. It is critical to break that downward cycle.

The best way to feel better is through moderate exercise—walking, jogging, swimming. Exercise also creates dopamine, the "feel-good" chemical in the brain. When exercising, dopamine produces a "runner's high" or "second wind." It's the most effective way to elevate serotonin levels, but it will take time. You will need to exercise for a few weeks before observing a noticeable improvement. Exercising with a friend may serve as motivation for each other.

Start slowly, adding more distance or more repetitions each day. If you must drag yourself down the street, get going! Even five minutes is better than nothing. When I started jogging, I could only make it as far as my mailbox. Gasping, I added a mailbox a day, and soon I was running three miles. Anything you consistently do for twenty-one days will become part of your routine. Determine to make yourself exercise every day.

I recommend working out in the morning. It will wake you up, energize you, and get your heart pumping. If you exercise too close to bedtime, you may not be able to sleep. You must sleep! Experts recommend forty minutes of aerobic exercise per day. Of course, people who exercise longer receive more benefits but try to work up to at least forty minutes. People who exercise daily become more decisive and more assertive. We want that to happen for you!

Hit the streets. Do not overdo it at first. Start slowly, build up your strength, and keep at it!

Diet: The Dreaded "D" Word

Unhappy people who are depressed may do impulsive things to lift their moods. They will eat too much food, spend too much money, or watch too much TV. They try to "treat" themselves. Their vampire mates attack them for these behaviors, they feel guilty, and the cycle continues to spiral downward. You would be surprised how much more control you will have when your serotonin levels are high.

You do not need "comfort food." You need strength. Assertively address your emotional needs. Food is not an emotional cure. Overeating will complicate the situation and your life. Food has no value in addressing emotional issues.

People diet to lose weight and look more attractive, but we want you to change your diet to be healthy. If you are overeating, healthy food choices help you lose weight. If you are not eating enough, healthy food choices will help you gain needed weight. We want you to be healthy and physically strong.

A balanced diet means getting the protein, energy, and nutrients you need. Almost any healthy diet will work. We are looking for a balanced diet that avoids empty calories. Stay away from unhealthy fats and oils, too many sweets, or processed foods. Fruits and vegetables are your friends. Resist foods that trigger overeating. When depressed, people may eat to feel better, but their lives are not better. We want you to improve your life, not trick your body into telling you what you want to hear.

I must warn you: Do not drink too much alcohol. Alcohol can serve as a drug that decreases anxiety and agitation, and it is a dangerous drug. Alcohol is a central nervous system depressant and slows down everything. It will only make you more depressed. Do not fall for it as a quick fix.

Alcohol will make you more impulsive, and you need to be on your toes for the battle you are waging. Although you may feel calmer when you drink, you are more likely to say something, do something, or agree to something you will regret later. You already know from living with a vampire that anything you say can and will be used against you. You want to avoid that at all costs. Marriage vampires take those unguarded remarks and shortsighted agreements and make you feel guilty if you don't follow through. Be alert. Say precisely what you need to say, and only make agreements you intend to keep. If you are tipsy, you will not be in control. You know not to drink and drive. You know not to drink and then fly an airplane. But most importantly, do not drink and talk to a vampire!

Laugh a Lot

Exercise releases endorphins (serotonin and dopamine), but guess what else releases these same chemicals in your brain? *Laughter!*

Typically, the wives of marriage vampires do not have much to laugh about, so you will have to search for it. Search for comedy TV shows or films. Listen to your favorite comedians, read a funny book, listen to an entertaining podcast while out for a walk, or watch cat memes—whatever makes you laugh. I'm not talking about smiles. I am talking about laughing out loud!

In his book, *Anatomy of an Illness as Perceived by a Patient*, Norman Cousins shares how he extended his life from a projected six months to eleven years through the actual physical impact the laughter had on his body. After receiving an incurable connective tissue disease diagnosis, Cousins decided he would watch comedy films he'd enjoyed in his youth during his treatment. Not only did his mood improve, but he found that ten minutes of laughter was worth an hour of pain medication due to the release of dopamine into his brain.

Watch anything that makes you laugh. Get together with good friends for a game or movie night and take time to talk and laugh. Take time to embrace the joy that life offers, even when times are difficult.

When Medication is Needed

If you are severely depressed, you may need medication prescribed under a physician's care. Different medications are available, but most are related. The most prescribed antidepressants are SSRI's—Selective Serotonin Re-uptake Inhibitors. They work by slowing down the absorption of serotonin back into the system. Your brain makes serotonin, bathes the nerves in your brain with it, then soaks it back up for use again. By slowing down its "re-uptake," the serotonin stays on your nerves longer. SSRIs are great for people who sleep too much, overeat, think too slowly, and feel lethargic. They may not address the symptoms of people who cannot sleep, have racing thoughts, feel agitated or suffer a loss of appetite. Work with your physician or psychiatrist to ensure your symptoms respond appropriately to the treatment prescribed.

There is no magic "happy pill." Medications may address your physical symptoms and may provide a lift in the mood for some people. Even if you take antidepressant medications, exercising, eating right, and sleeping right are still essential. Exercise, sleep, and healthy eating are all pro-active things you can do to help raise your serotonin levels. The first sign of increased serotonin is a little extra zip in the afternoon—look for it! When your serotonin levels rise in your body, your physician may decide it's time to decrease or discontinue your medications. *Never* decrease or discontinue your medications on your own.

A host of physical ailments also mimic depression and result in lethargy. Low thyroid, folate deficiency, anemia (low iron), and chronic fatigue syndrome look and feel like depression. However, they do not respond to antidepressant treatment. You will need to obtain a physical and have lab work done to determine if any of these complicate your goal of standing up for yourself.

Antidepressant meds take time, and you will not feel better right away. People will not feel any effect of SSRIs for a week or two. Do not become discouraged. Not every medication works on everybody. It may take time to find the one that is right for you. Collaborate closely with your doctor and follow their instructions.

Un-boggle Your Mind

Nothing is quite as stressful as constant criticism, ridicule, harassment, and a steady stream of put-downs from someone who is supposed to love you. It's downright mind-boggling that someone who claims to love a person would treat that person in that way.

To counter those jabs, read books that help you feel good about yourself. People have found relief from the book *Search for Significance* by Robert McGee. When I was working in a Christian in-patient hospital program called RAPHA, we gave each patient that book and workbook and used it as the basis of our program. The book was written to help people combat Satan's lies with God's truth.

Many books about boundaries and stress management exist. Find books you like. You will not agree with all of them; toss the ones you don't like. You can find one that speaks to you, is easy to read, and makes sense.

Of course, the obvious place for a Christian to go for help is to God's Word—the last Word on any problem you might have. When you read, be open to the entire text. Being raised in a fundamentalist church, we tended to skip the parts of the Bible that were hard to understand. Please read it all. The Bible speaks of the Spirit more than you may recall, and you will be delighted to find the wonderful things God has to say about you. I love to read Romans 8, Ephesians 6:10-20, Colossians 3:5-17, and all of I John. What passages speak to you, encourage, and comfort you?

If you have a history of finding verses that scare you to death or make you feel guilty, avoid those for a while. I once had a client who had underlined every verse that warns us of the consequences of sin. I told her to put that Bible aside and use another one to highlight all of God's promises and affirmations. She was stunned! The Bible is a book of love, a book of hope, and the path to success. Read it that way.

Find Your Fight Song!

Music sets the tone and rhythm of life. That is why they give an Academy Award for "Best Song." Music makes a significant difference in our energy levels, hearts, and minds. Every college has a fight song. Every nation has a patriotic anthem. Find your fight song. Listen to music that moves you, makes you feel determined, and reminds you of your worth. No matter the genre, find music that lifts your spirits.

Some good "fight songs" might include:

- "We are the Champions," by Queen
- "I Am Woman," by Helen Reddy
- "Survivor," Destiny's Child
- "Fight Song," by Rachel Platten
- "The Fight Is On," by Marion Williams
- "I Will Survive," by Gloria Gaynor
- "We Shall Overcome," by Pete Seeger
- "Get Up Offa That Thing," by James Brown
- "Let It Go," by Idina Menzel
- "Roar," by Katy Perry

Once, I worked at an exceedingly difficult job. On the drive home from work, I tuned in to an "oldies" radio station. Listening to that music put me in a good mood. I knew all the words to those songs and could sing along. Now, "oldies" are not as old these days, and I do not know all the lyrics, but I don't have that job anymore. Good songs can change your outlook quickly, especially if you sing along.

"...but be filled with the Spirit, addressing one another in psalms and hymns and spiritual songs, singing and making melody to the Lord with all your heart..." (Ephesians 5:18-19, RSV)

Make melody in your heart to God, no matter what your voice sounds like. If dogs howl when you croon, sing anyway. If you have a musical heritage, use it. If not, start one. All kinds of Christian albums will touch your heart—from Gregorian chants to rap, from Contemporary Christian Music to Tennessee Ernie Ford. Even Elvis had a gospel album.

Music can lift your mood while you cook, clean, or prepare for your vampire to come home and start complicating your life all over again. Singing can help you visualize something better and inspire you.

When David was king, he wrote a song about a lamb cared for by a shepherd. David thought of himself as a lamb beside still waters and led into green pastures. It was a more relaxing image than being a king expected to lead, who could never appear weak or indecisive, and whose own children wanted to kill him! He sang of God, making David the guest of honor at a banquet while all his critics had to watch. He sang of walking through the Valley of Death with no fear. (Psalms 23, RSV)

Can we sing about walking through the Valley of a Vampire, knowing we do not have to be sucked dry? Can we visualize being honored by God even though our "enemy" does not honor us? Can we see God taking care of us and leading us to a peaceful place?

Quit singing the blues. Quit living in silence. Play music that lifts you up and then sings the New You, aloud and with passion, no matter how loud the dog's howl!

Remember, at the end of the day, whether you stay or leave, the Lord is building godly character in you through these troubles. His end purpose is for you to have hope, hold your head high, and never be ashamed.

The Bible talks about these building blocks in Romans 5:3-5, ESV:

"More than that, we rejoice in our sufferings, knowing that suffering produces endurance, and endurance produces character, and character produces hope, and hope does not disappoint us, because God's love has been poured into our hearts through the Holy Spirit which has been given to us." (Romans 5:3-5, RSV)

11

Lean on Me

"Be transformed by the renewal of your mind."
(Romans 12:2, RSV)

At this point, as difficult as it may be to leave your spouse or to stay and tough it out, it will be worse if you choose to walk alone. Finding your support system may also be a challenge, but you will discover it is well worth the effort.

"Blessed be the God and Father of our Lord Jesus Christ, the Father of mercies and God of all comfort, who comforts us in all our affliction, so that we may be able to comfort those who are in any affliction, with the comfort with which we ourselves are comforted by God." (2 Corinthians 1:3-4, RSV)

It's important to talk about safety in numbers. When they went into battle, the Roman soldiers stood in a large, square formation, interlocking their shields at the perimeter, while the soldiers in the interior lifted their shields high above their heads. The group was virtually impenetrable, like one big tank slowly moving down the battlefield. I use this illustration as an example, so you know you weren't meant to "go it alone." I hope it helps you understand the power you have when engaged with the Body of Christ.

It is vital to get involved in a prayer group. People who are genuinely full of faith can undergird and lift you by their prayer efforts and support. These friends also need to be available and willing to help with practical needs you may have. It may be meals, childcare, or just a safe place when you need one. We need each other. This is part of your "shield of faith."

Different states or regions of the country will offer a variety of available resources, government-funded agencies, church-sponsored programs, counselors and therapists, or even victims of NPD. They may want to start their own groups.

Local therapists may be willing to guide you and facilitate your group. But before you invite a therapist to lead your group, you need to know what the therapist believes about personality disorders. How much experience has a therapist had to help people in relationships with marriage vampires (NPDs)? The therapist must also respect your beliefs and work within the group's religious framework.

Find a Perfect Fit

Read all the information you can find and learn as much as possible. There are all sorts of "takes" on what to do. Don't fall for the first suggestion or explanation you hear. Take it all in and review it thoroughly.

You have lived with this type of personality, and you will be able to perceive what rings true. Again, I ask you to trust yourself. If the book's author knows what they are talking about, you will know it. You will feel it at a gut level. It will make sense to you.

The Internet has ways to connect with others in similar situations but be careful. There are also angry wives and

ex-wives of mar-
riage vampires. Do
not let them infect
you with their anger
and hostility. Please
do not take their
wounds and wear
them yourself. En-
courage them to
heal and focus on
their new lives, free
from judgment, filled with blessings, and covered with
God's protection.

All support groups are not equal. Licensed, professional
therapists may offer group sessions. Groups may be com-
prised of peers and offer support. Other groups may be
leaderless. You may have to build a group, inviting others
you know who are like-minded or have had similar experiences. You may want to find a respected leader to lead
the group for you.

"...and let us consider how to stir up one another to love
and good works, not neglecting to meet together, as is the
habit of some, but encouraging one another, and all the
more as you see the Day drawing near." (Hebrews 10:24-
25, RSV)

Conclusion #1

Contrary to Christmas carols we've sung and teachings we
may have heard our entire lives, Christ does not offer or
teach that He came to bring peace on earth. He came to
bring peace to *YOU*! To your heart and mind!

Jesus said, "Do not think that I have come to bring peace
on earth; I have not come to bring peace, but a sword."
(Matthew 10:34, RSV)

He also said, "Peace I leave with you; my peace I give to
you; not as the world gives do I give to you. Let not your

hearts be troubled, neither let them be afraid." (John 14:27, RSV)

I wrote this book to bring a "sword"—the truth—to people locked in a relationship draining the life out of them. Jesus said He came that we might have life more abundantly, not a lifetime of being emotionally or physically battered by a creature that has no love in him.

This book is a call to arms!

I help people challenge the lies that have kept them confused and bound. You may have been struggling for years just to have a loving, caring marriage, only to find yourself in a no-win situation. Now you are simply hoping to survive. God does not call us to survival. He calls us to victory.

The things God says about you are true, whether you are married or single, happy or sad, tricked into a relationship with a narcissist, or with a stable, caring partner who loves you unconditionally.

The truth is the truth.

I am interested in speaking the truth and helping others see the power of knowing who they are, believing what is true, and identifying those who attempt to manipulate.

Once you see and understand the purpose of lies—to wound, punish, control, or get us to give in—you can interpret lies correctly. Now that you have armor, you can protect yourself against wounds. Once you see marriage vampires as they indeed are, you can develop strategies to nurture, heal, and protect yourself.

You may read this book and say, "It's not exactly me." But if you can read this book and use it to help yourself heal, you will never see a vampire as Prince Charming again. You will never see yourself as worthless or hopeless. The fact that you had no idea that vampires existed doesn't mean that you can't use the tools God has given you to fight and win.

I wrote this book to inspire hope. Psalms 68:6 says that God leads the "prisoners to prosperity." He does not lead them to survival but instead to abundance. God will lead you to strength, lead you to victory, and lead you to joy, but it will be a struggle. It is going to be a fight. It is going to take time. Take the challenge! Fight the battle! Win the victory!

There is light at the end of the tunnel. I have seen women who believed their lives were over, felt trapped forever, who then instead rose for battle and won.

Conclusion #2

I have seen women who at one point wouldn't look anyone in the eye change into powerful women living with their heads held high, not afraid of life's challenges. I have seen women who once believed no one would ever find them attractive again turn down relationships with handsome, successful men simply because these successful men reminded them of a vampire they had fought so hard to escape. They didn't want to take that risk. They had become so self-assured that they could turn down what looked like a good catch on the chance they might be an NPD. Previously, they could not have done that, but they'd become wiser and more discerning.

You may not have an experience like Barbie, Janice, Faith, or Laura, but I hope they inspire you. Fill yourself with God's hope, fill yourself with God's strength, and put on the whole armor of God. Take the sword of the Spirit and take God's path to freedom and spiritual prosperity.

My clients have me. You have this book. It is not the only book, and I am not the only therapist. The battle will be difficult, and you will need to be prepared. Evaluate your situation seriously; do not underestimate the task. Be prepared, realistic, and determined. Gather information, locate tools, and find the help and support you need. It will not be easy but do it anyway. Follow the path to victory and freedom!

You don't need your spouse to love you. You need to love yourself! God already does!

God will give you hope. God will give you strength! God gives you a path. It's up to you to take it. You can do it!

Recommended Reading

Anatomy of an Illness as Perceived by a Patient, Norman Cousins (ISBN-13: 9780553343656)

Malignant Self Love: Narcissism Revisited, Sam Vaknin (ISBN-13: 9788023833843)

Stop Walking on Eggshells, Paul T. Mason, Randi Kreger (ISBN-13: 9781452674070)

Help! I am in love with a Narcissist, Steven Carter, Julia Sokol (ISBN-13: 9781590770771)

When You Love a Man Who Loves Himself, W. Keith Campbell (ISBN-13: 9781402203428)

Tears and Healing: The Journey to the Light After an Abusive Relationship, Richard Skerritt (ISBN-13: 9781933369013)

The Search for Significance: Seeing Your True Worth Through God's Eyes, Richard McGee (ISBN-13: 9780849944246)

Why Is It Always About You? The Seven Deadly Sins of Narcissism, Sandy Hotchkiss (ISBN-13: 9780743214285)

About the Author

Plans are established by counsel;
by wise guidance wage war.
(Proverbs 20:18, RSV)

Clifton Fuller, LCSW-S, LPC-S, LMFT-S

Clifton Fuller is a counselor in private practice in San Antonio, TX. He holds a Bachelor of Science Degree in Psychology (B.S. Psychology) and a Master's Degree in Marriage and Family Therapy (M.M.F.T.). He graduated from Abilene Christian University with high honors in his under-graduate college work and the highest honors in his graduate studies.

Clifton Fuller is licensed in the State of Texas as a Texas Licensed Clinical Social Worker (LCSW), Texas Licensed Professional Counselor (LPC), and an LMFT (Texas Licensed Marriage and Family Therapist). He also holds Supervisor status in all three of those licensing areas.

He has worked in various mental health environments, making him uniquely qualified to counsel a wide range of clients of all ages.

He is the fifth of seven children, raised by a divorced mother who exhibited and taught her children about faith, values, and "what good husbands do." His father was an abusive alcoholic and a narcissist. His parents, family, educators, mentors, and church support networks influenced his future life opportunities and life decisions. His father came back from WWII as an angry, violent man who became an alcoholic and took the family into poverty. His mother supported the family, loving her husband, but recognizing his faults. As the family situation became more severe, she turned to her family and church for help, eventually realizing she had to leave her husband to protect her children. The family separated, living in multiple family members' homes until five of the children were placed in a children's home, where she later went to work. Clifton did not live with his mother from fifth grade until his junior year in high school.

Clifton does not want others to experience the childhood struggles he had to endure, but if they do, he wants them to realize the resiliency of human nature and what hope and decisions can do to move lives forward. He believes the challenges he faced as a child and teen made him stronger and helped him build his skills as a therapist today. His early life caused him to make a conscious choice to create a different type of marriage than the one he'd seen his parents have, to try to give his children opportunities he'd never had, and to try to prevent others from experiencing the traumas and difficulties he faced as a child.

He attended Abilene Christian University as they offered tuition assistance for children living at the children's home where he lived at the time. While in college, he held multiple jobs to pay the remaining costs not covered by lowered tuition.

He completed his undergraduate degree in three years and met his wife, who also attended ACU. They were married in 1973. He tells people that he'd never known what true happiness was until that time. He and his wife have two incredible sons and daughters-in-law, as well as precious grandchildren who enrich their lives.

After graduation, Clifton began his profession as a therapist and Director of Social Work at the childcare facility in rural Texas where he and his family had lived. The facility served emotionally disturbed children that child-protective services had removed from their homes, homeless children sponsored by a church, or children who needed care outside their home due to other situations.

Clifton and his family stayed there for years. However, when his sons were young, Clifton and his wife returned to Abilene Christian University, where he obtained his marriage and family therapy graduate degree.

When he moved to San Antonio, Texas, he initially accepted a position as a Family Counseling Coordinator in a hospital setting where he provided counseling for individuals and families who had a family member in the hospital's care. He later accepted a position in an in-patient psychiatric hospital as a therapist and director of multiple programs. Because San Antonio has many military bases, he found that a significant part of his work centered around the unique challenges military families face, as they protect our nation yet are asked to relocate frequently.

Programs he directed included: Drug and Alcohol Treatment programs (for both adolescents and adults), Co-Dependency Programs, an In-patient Christian Counseling program, RAPHA Christian Counseling programs, "work-hardening" program (for patients returning to work after injury), and group counseling programs.

He received requests to provide private counseling services and began his private practice gradually, eventually becoming full-time in 1991.

He has worked with many personality disorders, adoptive and post-adoptive families, and military families. His experience includes:

- Certification in EMDR therapy (Eye Movement Desensitization and Reprocessing), to treat clients addressing pain management, phobia, anxiety, PTSD (Post Traumatic Stress Disorder), and depression.

- Is a clinical member of A.A.M.F.T. (American Association for Marriage and Family Therapy)

- Provides counseling for Texas individuals and families.

- Counsels abused clients, crime victims, military, and first-responders who've suffered trauma after responding to critical events.

- Counseled children, adolescents, and adults in inpatient settings.

- Collaborates with therapists and physicians regarding mental health issues, trauma, pain management, and anxiety.

- Court-ordered counseling for clients (marital, custody, or anger management)

- Consults with attorneys requesting information to address personality disorder traits or mental health concerns about their clients.

- Confers with pastors, clergy, and church leaders to address staff or membership issues.

- Furnishes crisis, grief, and loss counseling to communities and schools.

- Guides business professionals regarding career changes.

- Provides tools to businesses regarding employer and employee conflicts.

Clifton has counseled many families, businesses, and churches in crisis. But some of the most challenging are those whose world has been turned upside down by a destructive narcissistic personality.

Families asked, "Why haven't we heard about these personality disorders? You must write a book to let people know these kinds of people are out there!" When Clifton explained he had dyslexia and didn't have the skills necessary to write such a book, they disagreed, challenged him, and emphasized the critical need to share the information. This book fulfills that need and clients' insistence it be written. It is the compilation of years of counseling and observing families and individuals (including himself) who have more strength than they realize, even with what, at the time, may seem like overwhelming disabilities, situations, or insurmountable roadblocks.

Please visit CliftonFullerCounseling.com for additional information about Clifton Fuller, blog articles, and resources on other mental health topics.